大学入試　レベル別英語長文問題
Solution（ソリューション） 最新テーマ編3 トップレベル

別冊問題　もくじ

制限時間25分／419 words／解答：本冊p.16

Read the following passage and answer the questions below.

Ecological systems are the products of the organisms that inhabit them. (1) All organisms, to greater or lesser degrees, interact continuously with their physical environment and with each other. In some cases, their impact on ecosystems may be disproportionate to their size. Elephants and other grazing animals have made the Serengeti plains what they are, from the characteristics of the grasses on which they tread to the chemical structure of the soil. Billions of years ago, photosynthetic bacteria* created the earliest form of the atmosphere as we know it — and, (i) not coincidentally, sparked the first Ice Age. All organisms have a constant and never-ending impact on their ecosystems.

In the long span of human history, the vast majority of environmental damage has occurred in only the past three centuries. Fueled by industrialization and modernization, humans have generated large volumes of certain gases, altered the acidity of rivers, used up underground water sources, introduced alien species, and (ii) impoverished landscapes as they extract and consume resources. Surprising numbers of species have been driven to extinction as human populations have grown worldwide. Human activity has clearly had an enormous effect on the natural environment.

Humans, however, are not unique in their power to reshape

environments locally or globally. Burrowing rodents**, for example, maintain vast grasslands rich in their favorite foods by continuously turning the soil and discouraging the growth of forests. Sheep, brought to Mexico with the European settlement, created their own grazing land through the action of their hooves on the soil. Then there are the (iii) not-so-humble roles of microbes, worms, and other invertebrates*** in soil formation and rejuvenation. Some plant species have redefined the conditions of natural selection for countless living things and geological processes alike. The lesson is that humans, in their effects on the environment, are (iv) on a par with many other organisms.

The key to comprehending environmental history is an understanding of the bonds that have formed between humans and other species, for these have generated co-evolutionary processes with their own logic and drive. In many ecosystems today, humans are the dominant species. But such dominance cannot exist apart from the systems and processes that sustain it. The effects of (2) environmental trauma are real, but they are a product of scale, not human exceptionalism. Although the human impact on the planet today is surely the result of human actions and behavior, this should never be confused with intention or control. Nature, much like human society, typically declines to follow the scripts we sometimes choose to write for it.

Notes :

photosynthetic bacteria* : bacteria that use sunlight to produce nutrients

burrowing rodents** : animals with strong sharp front teeth that dig holes, such as prairie dogs

invertebrates*** : living creatures that have no backbone

Q1. Translate the underlined part (1) into Japanese.

Q2. According to the first paragraph in this passage, the impact of "elephants and other grazing animals" and "photosynthetic bacteria" on their environments "may be disproportionate." What does "disproportionate impact" mean in this context? Explain in Japanese.

Q3. Choose the most appropriate meaning of the underlined words or phrases (i) — (iv).

(i) not coincidentally

A. as a result　　B. by chance

C. randomly　　D. unexpectedly

(ii) impoverished

A. deleted　　B. improved

C. increased　　D. weakened

(iii) not-so-humble

A. arrogant　　B. harmonious

C. key　　D. minor

(iv) on a par with

A. distinct from　　B. handicapped by

C. less than　　D. similar to

Q4. Which of the following (A, B, C or D) best summarizes the meaning of the final paragraph of this passage?

A. Humans have limited control over nature.

B. Humans have to join together with nature.

C. Humans must choose how to control natural environments.

D. Humans will continue to destroy nature.

Q5. The final paragraph includes the underlined part (2) environmental trauma to describe negative effects on nature. Which of the following (A, B, C or D) is NOT used as an example of "environmental trauma" in this passage?

A. air composition change

B. animal extinction

C. soil production

D. water quality change

問題 2

制限時間 25 分／490 words／解答：本冊 p.32

次の英文を読み、設問 1. ～ 8. に答えよ。

A striking feature of most, if not all, animal communication is the lack of a symbolic structure. Most of the complexity in animal communication can be explained by the fact that listeners are (1) <u>apt</u> at extracting information from signals, while the sender does not always intend to provide that information. Further analyses of the structure of animal communication need to take into account that both the acquisition and the performance of vocal behavior differ substantially between different taxa[注1]. In terrestrial mammals, the structure of the utterances is generally considered to be innate, [2] songbirds have to learn (based on innate biases) their species-specific songs. Some animals produce series of repetitions of the same sound (e.g., the croaking of a frog), whereas others utter strings of different notes, often composed into higher-order structures. The structure of both birdsong and humpback whale[注2] songs has been explored. One of the most elaborate singers among the songbirds, the nightingale, commands up to 200 song types, with each consisting of a succession of several elements or notes. [3], the song of a typical nightingale may have up to 1000 different elements. Thus, the number of combinatorial signals is effectively smaller than the elements which make up the signal. (4) <u>The same</u> appears to be true for humpback whales, and is strikingly different from human language, in which the number of words is orders of magnitude [5] the number of possible sentences. The most elaborate bird and whale song exploits two main devices: repetition of syllables or phrases, and sequencing of up to about seven separate units (perhaps iterated[注3]) into a single phrase, itself perhaps iterated. Most significantly, bird and whale songs are combinatorial but not semantically compositional in the sense that the elements that make up the utterances carry specific meaning.

Perplexingly, the utterances of nonhuman primates are much less (6) elaborate than that of songbirds or whales, with the notable exception of gibbon[注4] song, despite the fact that nonhuman primates do not simply utter signal calls, but rather bouts of several calls. The question is (a) whether such sequences can be described in terms of syntactical[注5] rules, and (b) whether they allow listeners to attribute differential meaning based on the combination of different call units. The first point can be largely refuted as sequences do not follow fully predictable patterns; instead, signal combinations can be described more appropriately in probabilistic terms. (7) There is, however, good evidence for the second point. Since most monkey and ape species have relatively small repertoires, this constraint may have favored listeners' abilities to process signal combinations. On the production side, it remains unclear whether the processes that give rise to heterotypic call sequences (i.e., successions of different call types) are fundamentally different from those that lead to series of the same call.

注1　taxa　taxon（分類単位）の複数形　注2　humpback whale　ザトウクジラ
注3　iterate　繰り返す　注4　gibbon　テナガザル
注5　syntactical　文法的な

1. 下線部（1）を置き換えるのに最もふさわしいものを①～④から１つ選べ。

①　excel　②　prone　③　good　④　liable

2. 空所［　2　］を補うのに最もふさわしいものを①～④から１つ選べ。

①　if　②　unless　③　even　④　while

3. 空所［　3　］を補うのに最もふさわしいものを①～④から１つ選べ。

①　Altogether　②　In contrast
③　Naturally　④　For once

4. 下線部（4）の内容として最もふさわしいものを①～④から１つ選べ。

①　歌を構成する要素の方が、歌の数よりも少ないこと。
②　歌を構成する要素の方が、歌の数よりも多いこと。
③　歌はより小さな構成要素の連続体から成り立っていること。
④　歌は同一の音声の繰り返しから成り立っていること。

5. 空所［　5　］を補うのに最もふさわしいものを①～④から１つ選べ。

①　more than　②　as many as
③　as little as　④　less than

6. 下線部（6）を置き換えるのに適さないものはどれか。答えを①～④から１つ選べ。

①　intricate　②　complex
③　sophisticated　④　meaningful

7. 下線部 (7) の内容として最もふさわしいものを①～④から１つ選べ。

① 霊長類の鳴き声には文法的な規則性が存在する証拠がある。

② 霊長類の鳴き声には文法的な規則性が存在しない証拠がある。

③ 霊長類は鳴き声の組み合わせによって意味を区別している証拠がある。

④ 霊長類は鳴き声の組み合わせによる意味の区別が出来ない証拠がある。

8. 本文の内容と合致するものとして最もふさわしいものを①～④から１つ選べ。

① Animal communication is generally considered to be based on a symbolic system.

② Different animals undergo different processes in acquiring their communication systems.

③ Bird songs are similar to human language in that both exploit a combinatorial device to produce a virtually unlimited number of signals.

④ Whale songs are different from human language in that only the latter has the ability to combine separate units into a single phrase.

問題 3

制限時間25分／470 words／解答：本冊p.46

次の文章を読んで、問1～問4に答えなさい。

(1) Nature is like granola: The list of ingredients is long, but the bowl is mostly filled with just a few of them. Take England, for example, which is obsessed enough with animals and birds to count its wildlife nearly one by one, population estimates for 58 species of land mammal in that country, ranging from the familiar to the obscure, total about 173 million animals. But just three species — the common shrew*, rabbit, and mole — account for half of those individuals. All told, the most common 25 percent of English mammal species add up to 97 percent of all the individual animals. Similar patterns play out on land and at sea, in your local park or across whole continents, and whether you are counting beetles, shellfish, or tropical trees. The most common land bird in the United States and Canada is the American robin, harbinger of spring*. Robins alone are as numerous as the two countries' 277 least-common bird species combined.

The fact that species of such incredible abundance can decline as quickly as the white-rumped vulture did points to (2) a counter-intuitive idea in conservation that (3) common species may need protection just as much as rare ones do.

The first scientist to propose the conservation of the common was, almost too perfectly, the author of a book called *Rarity*. After 20 years of studying what made some species rare, Kevin Gaston, an ecologist at the University of Exeter, in England, started to wonder why other species are widespread and abundant. He soon came to a seemingly contradictory conclusion: "The state of being common is rare." While any given common species is made up of many individuals, only a small fraction of species are common.

Gaston's work culminated in "Common Ecology," a paper published in the journal BioScience in 2011 that found that commonness was not a well-studied phenomenon, and that "(A)." The work triggered a quiet increase in research. A study from 2014 hints at the scale of what has been overlooked. Its authors found that (B), and that (C).

(4) Industrial agriculture carries much of the blame for Europe's disappearing birds. "They've been taking out hedgerows, taking out trees, making fields bigger, increasing inputs of pesticides* — just essentially squeezing out the opportunities for wild organisms to live in those kinds of environments," Gaston told me. "We're talking just massive losses."

But even the most human-adapted and urban of birds, such as starlings* and house sparrows, have steeply decreased — in fact, those two very common birds were among the top five birds experiencing population declines. Most of the rarest birds in Europe are actually increasing at present, due to successful conservation efforts, although they remain uncommon; meanwhile, most of the common birds are declining toward scarcity. "The inevitable place you end up," said Gaston, "is that (D)."

注

shrew　トガリネズミ　　　harbinger of spring　春告げ鳥

pesticides　農薬　　　starling　ムクドリ

問1　下線部（1）の意味を、50字以内の日本語で、本文の内容に即して具体的に説明しなさい。ただし、句読点も1字に数えます。

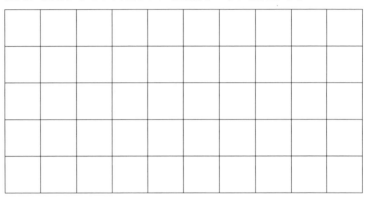

問2　下線部（2）を置き換えるのに最も適切な一続きの語句を、本文中から抜き出しなさい。

問3　下線部（3）と（4）を、それぞれ日本語に訳しなさい。

問4 空欄（ A ）～（ D ）に入る最も適切な表現を次の中からそれぞれ１つ選び、記号で答えなさい。ただし、同じ記号は一度しか使えません。

（あ） everything is rare

（い） many common species are as poorly studied as many rare ones

（う） the number of birds nesting in Europe has dropped by 421 million — fully one-fifth of the continent's bird population, gone — since 1980

（え） the species has recovered

（お） this decline in sheer birdiness is accounted for almost entirely by common species, among them such household names as the skylark

問題 4

制限時間25分／549 words／解答：本冊p.60

次の文章を読んで、(1)～(10)の設問に最適な答えを(a)～(d)から1つ選びなさい。

In the (1) hierarchy of human needs, good health is right at the top. There's a reason we say, "to your health," whenever we clink glasses.

In the complicated world of politics, therefore, with numerous (2) (　　) issues coming at us 24 hours a day, it's not surprising that concerns clearly relevant to our health and that of our families regularly rise to the top of our society's priority list. The effect of plastic on our health should be at the top of that list today.

As Bruce Lourie and I explain in our book Slow Death by Rubber Duck, once an issue transforms into a human health concern, it becomes far more likely to be taken up by our elected leaders, noticed by the general public and consequently solved.

The smoking debate followed this path. Once the focus became the damaging effects of second-hand smoke, i.e., it's not just the health of smokers at risk but the health of all those around them, (4) the momentum for change became impossible for even the most defiant cigarette companies to resist.

What we are witnessing now is the genesis of another human health problem that I believe has the potential to dominate public debate over the next decade: the discovery that tiny plastic particles are (5) permeating every human on earth.

Plastic, it turns out, never really disappears. In response to time and sunlight, or the action of waves, it just gets mushed into smaller and smaller bits. These microscopic particles then enter the food chain, air and soil. In the past couple of years, scientists have started to find these particles in an astonishing range of products including table salt and honey, bottled and tap water, shellfish and ... beer. In one recent study, 83 per cent of tap water in seven countries was found to contain plastic micro-fibres.

When the snow melts in Canada to reveal a winter's worth of Tim Hortons' cups and lids, every person in this country notices the plastic litter that surrounds us. Many of us know of the vast and accumulating patches of garbage in the ocean. I hear shoppers in the produce aisles of my local grocery store grumbling at the increasing size of the plastic that encases the organic arugula.

None of this, really, matters much. Do I care that sea turtles are choking to death on the plastic grocery bags I use every day? (7)(　　). But certainly not enough to inconvenience myself.

But if it turns out that my two boys have a dramatically increased chance of contracting prostate cancer because of all the plastic particles that are implanted in their growing bodies, now you've got my attention. Make it stop, please.

Forget recycling. We can't recycle ourselves out of this problem. The issue is our society's addiction to plastic itself. Those plastic micro-fibres I mentioned? Scientists are now saying that one of the primary sources in our drinking water is the lint that comes off the synthetic fabric of our clothing. It's not just the plastic we're throwing away that's the problem; it's the plastic items we surround ourselves with every day.

The new science on plastic micro-particles is stunning and I'm guessing (10) only the tip of a toxic iceberg.

(1) The word (1) hierarchy in this sentence most likely means ( ).

(a) a method of controlling alcohol consumption in human beings
(b) a system in which things are arranged by their importance
(c) a formula for determining different levels of success for humans
(d) a state of disorder resulting from human greed rather than need

(2) Based on the context in paragraph 2, select the word that best fits in (2) ( ).

(a) competing (b) agreeable
(c) interrupting (d) purposeful

(3) In paragraph 3, the author suggests that solutions to important issues become possible when these issues ( ).

(a) alter the lives of influential politicians in a direct manner
(b) change public perception through the input of local doctors
(c) are presented as affecting humanity in an unfavorable way
(d) are discussed in books such as Slow Death by Rubber Duck

(4) Based on the context in paragraph 4, the probable meaning of the underlined sentence (4) is that cigarette companies (　　).

(a) successfully opposed the movement
(b) eventually had to give in to change
(c) effectively maintained the status quo
(d) aggressively supported this reform

(5) In paragraph 5, the word (5) permeating most likely means (　　).

(a) punishing　　(b) entering
(c) controlling　　(d) frustrating

(6) In paragraph 6, which of the following is **NOT** true?

(a) These particles were discovered in only a limited number of products.
(b) Despite lengthy exposure to water, plastics do not mineralize or go away.
(c) In some countries most of the tap water was polluted with these particles.
(d) Plastic particles can be so minute that they are invisible to the naked eye.

(7) Based on the content in paragraphs 7 and 8, select the answer that is most suitable for (7) (　　).

(a) Never　　(b) Sort of
(c) Not really　　(d) Rather

(8) In paragraphs 7 to 9, the author seems to suggest that, due to inconvenience, people tend to avoid taking action on the plastics issue, except in the case where (　　).

(a) the plastic litter (trash) is revealed after the snow melts
(b) research confirms that organic foods will be unsafe to eat
(c) evidence shows that it will seriously impact loved ones
(d) the plastic in the ocean becomes too enormous to ignore

(9) In paragraph 10, what, according to the author, is the solution to this enormous problem?

(a) We should invest more funds in developing better recycling technology.

(b) We must prohibit clothing manufacturers from using synthetic materials.

(c) We should create storage units for the proper disposal of plastic goods.

(d) We must ultimately put an end to the production and use of plastic.

(10) What does the author mean by the phrase (10) only the tip of a toxic iceberg in the context of this sentence?

(a) That the solution to this issue is unreachable due to its height.

(b) That this new science on micro-particles is rather impressive.

(c) That this information is a minute part of a destructive whole.

(d) That tips of icebergs provide clues to containing this problem.

問題 5

制限時間25分／541 words／解答：本冊 p.76

次の英文を読み、下記の設問に答えよ。

【　あ　】

Middle-aged and older people who live sedentary lives are up to two and a half times more likely to die early, researchers said. (A)たとえ座っていることが、立っていることや歩いていることによって中断されたとしても、そのリスクは残った。

Light activity such as cooking or washing-up could help lessen the risk. People who did regular physical activity of any intensity were about five times less likely to die early than those who were not physically active.

The study, in The BMJ, analysed existing research on physical activity and mortality in nearly（　i　）adults aged（　ii　）and older. Participants had an average age of（　iii　）and were followed for an average of just under six years, during which time（　iv　）died.

Their activity levels were monitored at the start of the research using devices that track physical movements and were categorised into "light intensity" such as slow walking, "moderate activity" such as brisk walking, vacuuming or mowing the lawn and "vigorous activity" such as jogging or digging.

After adjusting for potential influencing factors, researchers found that any level of physical activity was associated with a substantially lower risk of early death.

Deaths (イ) as total activity increased, before levelling off. People who did light intensity activity for about five hours a day, or moderate to vigorous activity for 24 minutes a day had the most health benefits.

There were approximately five times as many deaths among the 25 per cent of least active people compared with the 25 per cent most active.

Researchers looked separately at sedentary behaviour and found sitting still for nine and a half hours or more was linked to a higher risk of early death. The most sedentary people, who spent an average of nearly ten hours a day sitting, were at a 163 per cent higher risk of dying before they might have been expected to during the period of the study than the least sedentary, who sat for an average of seven and a half hours.

Ulf Ekelund, of the Norwegian School of Sport Sciences in Oslo, who led the research, said: “Our findings provide clear scientific evidence that higher levels of total physical activity, (ロ) intensity, and less sedentary time are associated with lower risk of premature mortality in middle-aged and older people.”

Researchers from Germany and New Zealand said that the study was an important addition to existing knowledge but could not explain whether the distribution of activity across the day or week was relevant.

They added: “The clinical message seems straightforward: every step counts and even light activity is (ハ).”

Commenting on the research, Jess Kuehne, of the Centre for Ageing Better, said: "If we want to be healthy and (二) when we grow older, we need to do much more in our forties and fifties. As well as aerobic exercise like taking brisk walks, cycling or swimming, we also need to be boosting the strength in our muscles and bones and improving our balance. It's not just about adding years to our life, it's about adding life to our years and increasing the time that we stay fit, healthy and free from long-term health conditions or disability."

注 sedentary = requiring a sitting posture

設問1. 空所〔あ〕を埋めるのにもっとも適当なものを (a) ～ (d) から1つ選びなさい。

(a) Lower rates of early death are reported among middle-aged adults who exercise at least five days a week.

(b) Sitting still for nine and a half hours a day raises the risk of early death, a study has found.

(c) The results of recent research suggest that moderate exercise is more beneficial for health than light or vigorous physical activities.

(d) Young people do not exercise enough and spend almost 10 hours a day sitting, concludes a recent scientific report.

設問2. 空所（ｉ）～（iv）を埋めるのにもっとも適当な数字の組み合わせを（a）～（d）から１つ選びなさい。

(a)　（ｉ）2,149　（ii）62　（iii）40　（iv）36,400
(b)　（ｉ）36,400　（ii）40　（iii）62　（iv）2,149
(c)　（ｉ）36,400　（ii）62　（iii）40　（iv）2,149
(d)　（ｉ）2,149　（ii）40　（iii）62　（iv）36,400

設問3. 空所（イ）～（ニ）を埋めるのにもっとも適当なものを（a）～（d）からそれぞれ１つ選びなさい。

（イ）
(a) fell steeply　(b) increased moderately
(c) remained unchanged　(d) soared dramatically

（ロ）
(a) according to　(b) based on
(c) due to　(d) regardless of

（ハ）
(a) beneficial　(b) diagnostic
(c) extensive　(d) harmful

（ニ）
(a) affluent　(b) cheerful
(c) independent　(d) responsible

設問4. 下線部（A）「たとえ座っていることが、立っていることや歩いていることによって中断されたとしても、そのリスクは残った」を〔　　〕の中の語を並べ替えて英語に直しなさい。なお、解答はThe riskから始めること。
〔broken / by / if / remained / the risk / even / and / up / sitting / standing / walking / was / , / . 〕

問題 6

制限時間25分／546words／解答：本冊p.92

次の英文を読んで、以下の設問に答えなさい。

Everyone knows that we Brits treat our dogs better than our children, and we are often reminded that the Society for the Prevention of Cruelty to Animals (SPCA) was founded in 1824, sixty years before the National Society for the Prevention of Cruelty to Children. Is it deeply meaningful that the SPCA went on to become the Royal Society (RSPCA) while the children's society still waits for (a) <u>that honor</u>?

What, then, lies behind this remarkable but apparently sincere attachment we have to our dogs? The truth is, we seem more able to freely express ourselves with animals than we are with other people. Kate Fox, the British social commentator, pondering on (b) <u>this aspect</u> of the Brits' relationship with their pets, explains convincingly, "unlike our fellow Englishmen, animals are not embarrassed or put off by our un-English displays of emotion."

The word dog itself is peculiarly native to Britain and comes from an obscure Old English past. The alternative Germanic term, hound, refers mainly to hunting dogs. In feudal society, such dogs might be given special treatment by their lordly master and be fed from his table. But lesser dogs out in the yard had a rougher time, and our language is crammed with phrases suggesting that a dog's life, at least up to the nineteenth century, was a miserable fate: dog-tired, dogsbody, going to the dogs, die like a dog, and so on. For the most part, dogs were treated with contempt and sometimes cruelty. Even the question, "What was it like?" might produce the answer, "(c) An absolute dog!" No positive qualities here, then.

(d) In curious contrast, the modern reality is that the British treat dogs with huge affection, looking on them as beloved companions and having lifelong bonds with them. The British adore the legendary image of a dog's faithfulness and literal (i) doggedness.

Nature seems to provide plenty of evidence to justify this attitude. Endless anecdotes suggest that dogs are strangely and deeply (ii) attuned to their owners, with some observers believing their pets have (e) psychic powers. The researcher and scientist Rupert Sheldrake, for example, has conducted surveys to demonstrate that dogs (among other pets) waiting at home know the moment their owners leave the office and begin their homeward journey.

So what is a British dog's life like these days? Some commentators think the sense of (f) the phrase has gradually changed and now means to have a cosseted and comfortable existence, rather than the opposite. I am quite sure the Queen's corgis would agree with that.

However, this cozy impression is not (iii) borne out by our behavior in the real world. According to a 2013 survey, the (iv) incidence of stray and abandoned dogs in England was estimated at around 111,000.

What's going on here? Two extremes of behavior meeting in a confused national psyche? It does seem that, in their attitudes to animals and children, we find one of the paradoxes of the British temperament.

All the same, there is one common expression which continues to suggest a bond between human and animal that is more than mere friendship: "Love me, love my dog." Or rather, in practice, "Love my dog, love me." Watch dog owners meeting in a public park and you will see (g) how it works. Better than a dating agency any time.

設問(1) 本文中の下線部(a) that honorが指し示す内容を日本語で書きなさい。

設問(2) 本文中の下線部(b) this aspectが指し示す内容を日本語で書きなさい。

設問(3) 本文中の下線部(c) An absolute dog!はこの会話においてどのような意味を表しているか、本文中に述べられていることに基づいて日本語で答えなさい。

設問(4) 本文中の下線部(d) In curious contrastという表現で対比されている2つの事実を日本語で説明しなさい。

設問(5) 本文中の下線部(e) psychic powersとはどのような能力のことか、本文中に挙げられている具体例を用いて日本語で説明しなさい。

設問(6) 本文中の下線部(f) the phraseが指し示すものを**英語で**答えなさい。

設問(7) 本文中の下線部(g) how it worksは、この後どのようになっていくことを暗示しているか日本語で述べなさい。

設問(8) 本文中の下線部(ⅰ)~(ⅳ)の語句に最も意味の近いものを(イ)~(ニ)から1つ選び、記号で答えなさい。

(ⅰ) doggedness
(イ) friendliness　(ロ) persistence
(ハ) pertinence　(ニ) wildness

(ⅱ) attuned to
(イ) attributed to　(ロ) correlated with
(ハ) in harmony with　(ニ) in submission to

(ⅲ) borne out
(イ) conveyed　(ロ) modified
(ハ) produced　(ニ) supported

(ⅳ) incidence
(イ) accident　(ロ) number
(ハ) occasion　(ニ) recurrence

問題 7

制限時間25分／555words／解答：本冊p.106

次の英文を読み、設問に答えなさい。

We are in the midst of a crisis of massive proportions and ①grave global significance. No, I do not mean the global economic crisis that began in 2008. At least then everyone knew that a crisis was at (1), and many world leaders worked quickly and desperately to find solutions. Indeed, consequences for governments were profound if they did not find solutions, and many were replaced in consequence. No, I mean a crisis that goes largely unnoticed, (A) a cancer; a crisis that is likely to be, in the long run, far more damaging to the future of democratic self-government: a worldwide crisis in education.

Radical changes are occurring in what democratic societies teach the young, and these changes have not been well thought through. Thirsty for national profit, nations, and their systems of education, are heedlessly discarding skills that are needed to keep democracies alive. If this trend continues, nations all over the world will soon be producing generations of useful machines, rather than complete citizens who can think for themselves, criticize tradition, and understand the significance of another person's sufferings and achievements. The future of the world's democracies ②hangs in the balance.

What are these radical changes? The humanities and the arts are being cut away, in both primary/secondary and college/university education, in virtually every nation of the world. Seen by policy-makers as useless frills, at a time when nations must cut away all useless things in order to stay competitive in the global market, they are rapidly losing their place in curricula, and also in the minds and hearts of parents and children. Indeed, what we might call the humanistic aspects of science and social science — the imaginative, creative aspect, and the aspect of rigorous critical thought — are losing ground as nations prefer to pursue short-term profit by the ③cultivation of the useful and highly applied skills suited to profit-making.

This crisis is facing us, but we have not yet faced it. We go on as if everything were business as usual, when in reality great changes of emphasis are evident all over. We haven't really thought hard (B) these changes, we have not really chosen them, and yet they increasingly limit our future.

(X), especially at this time of crisis, too few questions have been (2) about the direction of education, and, with it, of the world's democratic societies. With the rush to profitability in the global market, values precious for the future of democracy, especially in an era of religious and economic anxiety, are in danger of getting lost.

The profit motive suggests to many concerned leaders that science and technology are of crucial importance for the future health of their nations. We should have no (3) to good scientific and technical education, and I shall not suggest that nations should stop trying to improve in this regard. My concern is that other abilities, equally crucial, are at risk of getting lost in ④<u>the competitive flurry</u>, abilities crucial to the health of any democracy internally, and to the creation of a decent world culture capable of constructively addressing the world's most (4) problems.

These abilities are associated with the humanities and the arts: the ability to think critically; the ability to transcend local loyalties and to approach world problems as a "citizen of the world"; and, finally, the ability to imagine sympathetically the predicaments of another person.

[1] 下線部①～④の意味の説明として最も適切なものを選択肢１～４から選びなさい。

① 1. serious 2. small 3. snappy 4. sneaky

② 1. is bright 2. is doomed
3. is hopeful 4. is uncertain

③ 1. basement 2. development
3. judgment 4. payment

④ 1. the race for military superiority
2. the race for money and power
3. the race to win students
4. the race to win votes

[2] 空所（　1　）～（　4　）に入る最も適切な語を選択肢1～4の中から選びなさい。

(1)　1. hand　2. most　3. noon　4. once

(2)　1. ask　2. posed　3. replaced　4. voice

(3)　1. correction　2. objection
　3. rejection　4. suggestion

(4)　1. negligible　2. pollution
　3. pressing　4. trivial

[3] 次の1～7の語(句)を文法的・内容的に最も適切な順序に並べかえて（　X　）を完成させたとき、3番目にくるものの番号と、5番目にくるものを答えなさい。なお、文頭にくる語の一文字目も小文字にしてある。

1. all　2. given　3. growth
4. is so eagerly　5. nations　6. sought by
7. that economic

[4] （　A　）と（　B　）に入る最も適切な語を選択肢1～8の中から選びなさい。

1. about　2. at　3. besides　4. however
5. like　6. moreover　7. that　8. whereupon

[5] 本文の内容を最も適切に表現する表題をつけたい。選択肢1～4から選びなさい。

1. The Fake Crisis　2. The Financial Crisis
3. The Silent Crisis　4. The Visible Crisis

[6] 英文の内容に一致するものを選択肢1～8から3つ選びなさい。

1. The radical changes occurring in educational systems around the world are a result of thorough consideration.
2. We should cut away the sciences and devote more resources to the humanities and arts.
3. Cutting the humanities and arts from education is likely to have harmful consequences for the health of democracies.
4. Being able to put your feet in other people's shoes is a key skill connected with the humanities and arts.
5. The humanities and arts are being cut away, but students are fully aware of their importance.
6. There was a worldwide economic crisis which started in 2008.
7. Local traditions are undesirable and should be transcended.
8. Nations today tend not to put enough emphasis on profitability.

問題 8

制限時間20分／519 words／解答:本冊p.122

Read the following three passage and mark the most appropriate choice (a ~ d) for each item (1 ~ 5) on the separate answer sheet.

We animals are the most complicated things in the known universe. The universe that we know, of course, is a tiny fragment of the actual universe. There may be yet more complicated objects than us on other planets, and some of them may already know about us. But this doesn't alter the point that I want to make. Complicated things, everywhere, deserve a very special kind of explanation. We want to know how they came into existence and why they are so complicated. The explanation, as I shall argue, is likely to be broadly the same for complicated things everywhere in the universe; the same for us, for chimpanzees, worms, oak trees and monsters from outer space. On the other hand, it will not be the same for what I shall call 'simple' things, such as rocks, clouds, rivers, galaxies and quarks. These are the stuff of physics. Chimps and dogs and bats and cockroaches and people and worms and dandelions and bacteria and galactic aliens are the stuff of biology.

The difference is one of complexity of design. Biology is the study of complicated things that give the appearance of having been designed for a purpose. Physics is the study of simple things that do not tempt us to invoke design. At first sight, man-made artefacts like computers and cars will seem to provide exceptions. They are complicated and obviously designed for a purpose, yet they are not alive, and they are made of metal and plastic rather than of flesh and blood. In my view they should be firmly treated as biological objects.

The reader's reaction to this may be to ask, 'Yes, but are they really biological objects?' Words are our servants, not our masters. For different purposes we find it convenient to use words in different senses. Most cookery books class lobsters as fish. Zoologists can become quite upset about this, pointing out that lobsters could with greater justice call humans fish, since fish are far closer kin to humans than they are to lobsters. And, talking of justice and lobsters, I understand that a court of law recently had to decide whether lobsters were insects or 'animals' (it bore upon whether people should be allowed to boil them alive). Zoologically speaking, lobsters are certainly not insects. They are animals, but then so are insects and so are we. There is little point in getting worked up about the way different people use words (although in my nonprofessional life I am quite prepared to get worked up about people who boil lobsters alive). Cooks and lawyers need to use words in their own special ways. Never mind whether cars and computers are 'really' biological objects. The point is that if anything of that degree of complexity were found on a planet, we should have no hesitation in concluding that life existed, or had once existed, on that planet. Machines are the direct products of living objects; they derive their complexity and design from living objects, and they are diagnostic of the existence of life on a planet. The same goes for fossils, skeletons and dead bodies.

1 Dandelions and worms
(a) are complicated in the same way as humans or even aliens from outer space are.
(b) can be found all across the known universe.
(c) may appear to be complicated but in fact they are very simple, like rocks and clouds.
(d) need to be discussed and explained separately from other complex living things.

2 It is the author's belief that complicated things, such as cars or computers,
(a) are not of interest because they were designed for a specific purpose.
(b) may be discussed as being a part of biology even though they are not alive.
(c) really belong to the study of physics.
(d) should be considered as distinct from the study of biology.

3 Scientists who specialise in the study of animals
(a) believe that humans are more closely related to lobsters than they are to fish.
(b) have reached a consensus that lobsters should be classified as a type of insect.
(c) now understand that insects must never be considered as animals.
(d) would not accept lobsters being described as fish.

4 According to the author,

(a) language and vocabulary are clearly both biological objects.

(b) lawyers and cooks are examples of professionals who do not use words carefully.

(c) the meaning of any word is sacred and should never be altered.

(d) words are tools that we can adapt to best suit our immediate purpose.

5 Machines are said to be an indication of the existence of life because

(a) several complex machines have been found on other planets.

(b) some form of life would be necessary to initiate the complex design of a machine.

(c) these complex mechanical objects are predicted to replace biological life in the future.

(d) they are often found in places where there are no fossils, skeletons, or dead bodies.

Read the text and answer the following questions.

[A] The uniqueness of a work of art is inseparable from its being part of the fabric of tradition. This tradition itself is thoroughly alive and extremely changeable. An ancient statue of Venus, for example, stood in a different traditional context with the Greeks, who made it an object of worship, than with the priests of the Middle Ages, who viewed it as a frightening idol. They both, however, had to face up to its uniqueness, that is, its aura. We know that the earliest art works originated in the service of a ritual — first the magical, then the religious kind. It is significant that the existence of the work of art with reference to its aura was never entirely separated from its ritual function. In other words, the unique value of the "authentic" work of art has its basis in ritual.

[B] This ritualistic basis, however remote, is still recognizable even in the most irreligious forms of the cult of beauty. However this secular cult of beauty, developed during the Renaissance and prevailing for three centuries, clearly showed how art's ritualistic basis was declining. With the discovery of the first truly revolutionary means of reproduction, photography, simultaneously with the rise of socialism, art sensed the approaching crisis which has become evident a century later. At the time, art reacted with the doctrine of "art for art's sake." This gave rise to the idea of "pure" art, which not only denied any social function of art but also any categorizing by subject matter.

[C] An analysis of art in the age of mechanical reproduction leads us to an all-important insight: for the first time in world history, mechanical reproduction frees the work of art from its dependence on ritual. From a photographic negative, for example, one can make any number of prints; to ask for the "authentic" print makes no sense. But the instant the standard of authenticity ceases to be applicable to artistic production, the total function of art is reversed. Instead of being based on ritual, it begins to be based on another practice: politics.

[D] Works of art are received and valued on different levels. Two opposite types stand out; with one, the accent is on the cult value; with the other, on the exhibition value of the work. Artistic production begins with ceremonial objects destined to serve in a cult. One may assume that what mattered was their existence, not their being on view. The deer portrayed by the man of the Stone Age on the walls of his cave was an instrument of magic. He did expose it to his fellow men, but in the main it was meant for the spirits. Today the cult value would seem to demand that the work of art remain hidden. Certain statues of gods are accessible only to the priest in the temple; certain sculptures on medieval cathedrals are invisible to the spectator on ground level. When these various art practices are freed from ritual, the opportunities for exhibition of their products are increased. It is easier to exhibit a portrait bust that can be sent here and there than to exhibit the statue of a god that has its fixed place in the interior of a temple. The same holds for the painting as against the mosaic or fresco that preceded it.

(1) Which of the following ideas cannot be found in paragraph [A] ?

① Tradition can be compared to cloth.
② Magic and religion belong to different periods of history.
③ Works of art were part of a ceremony in earlier periods.
④ Art works must be a mixture of the beautiful and the fearful.

(2) Which of the following ideas can be found in paragraph [B] ?

① The ritualistic element of art remains always unchanged.
② A ritualistic element of art can be found even when the art work is not religious.
③ The ritualistic element of art remained unchanged until the invention of photography.
④ Many socialist ideas can be compared to the technique of photography.

(3) In paragraph [B] we find the phrase, "the idea of 'pure' art, which not only denied any social function of art but also any categorizing by subject matter." Which of the following best restates the meaning of that phrase?

① The idea that art is of some use to society, but only if it is about something specific.
② The idea that art is of some use to society, but only if the artist thinks it is.
③ The idea that art is of no use to society and does not have to be about anything in particular.
④ The idea that only art can really be of use to society in any category.

(4) Which of the following best summarizes the content of paragraph [C] ?

① Once art was mechanically reproduced, its role was completely changed.

② Once photographs were invented, there was no need for works of art.

③ Photography completely changed the rituals of politics.

④ Art became free from ritual, but only in a negative way.

(5) Which of the following best expresses the role of animal paintings in caves as explained in paragraph [D] ?

① Their function was mainly supernatural, although they could be viewed by humans.

② They were mainly to be viewed by humans, although they could have a supernatural function.

③ They could be viewed by humans, but only by using magical instruments.

④ They could be viewed by the spirits using magical instruments.

問題 10

制限時間25分／565 words／解答：本冊p.152

次の文章を読み、下の設問 1 ～ 3 に答えなさい。

Various doctrines of human cognitive superiority are made plausible by a comparison of human beings and the chimpanzees. For questions of evolutionary cognition, this focus is one-sided. Consider the evolution of cooperation in social insects, such as the Matabele ant. After a termite attack, these ants provide medical services. Having called for help by means of a chemical signal, injured ants are brought back to the nest. Their increased chance of recovery benefits the entire colony. Red forest ants have the ability to perform simple arithmetic operations and to convey the results to other ants.

When it comes to adaptations in animals that require sophisticated neural control, evolution offers (a) other spectacular examples. The banded archerfish is able to spit a stream of water at its prey, compensating for refraction at the boundary between air and water. It can also track the distance of its prey, so that the jet develops its greatest force just before impact. Laboratory experiments show that the banded archerfish spits on target even when the trajectory of its prey varies. Spit hunting is a technique that requires the same timing used in throwing, an activity otherwise regarded as unique in the animal kingdom. In human beings, the development of throwing has led to an enormous further development of the brain. And the archerfish? The calculations required for its extraordinary hunting technique are based on the interplay of about six neurons. Neural mini-networks could therefore be much more widespread in the animal kingdom than previously thought.

Research on honeybees has brought to light the cognitive capabilities of (b) minibrains. Honeybees have no brains in the real sense. Their neuronal density, however, is among the highest in insects, with roughly 960 thousand neurons — far fewer than any vertebrate. Even if the brain size of honeybees is normalized to their body size, their relative brain size is lower than most vertebrates. Insect behavior should be less complex, less flexible, and less modifiable than vertebrate behavior. But honeybees learn quickly how to extract pollen and nectar from a large number of different flowers. They care for their young, organize the distribution of tasks, and, with the help of the waggle dance, they inform each other about the location and quality of distant food and water.

Early research by Karl von Frisch suggested that such abilities cannot be the result of inflexible information processing and rigid behavioral programs. Honeybees learn and they remember. The most recent experimental research has, in confirming this conclusion, created an astonishing picture of the honeybee's cognitive competence. Their representation of the world does not consist entirely of associative chains. It is far more complex, flexible, and integrative. Honeybees show context-dependent learning and remembering, and even some forms of concept formation. Bees are able to classify images based on such abstract features as bilateral symmetry and radial symmetry; they can comprehend landscapes in a general way, and spontaneously come to classify new images. They have recently been promoted to the set of species capable of social learning and tool use.

(c) In any case, the much smaller brain of the bee does not appear to be a fundamental limitation for comparable cognitive processes, or at least their performance. The similarities between mammals and bees are astonishing, but they cannot be traced to homologous neurological developments. As long as the animal's neural architecture remains unknown, we cannot determine the cause of their similarity.

1 下線部 (a) の具体例として、このパラグラフではテッポウウオが獲物に水を噴射して狩りをする能力が紹介されている。その能力の特長を3点、日本語で箇条書きにしなさい。

2 下線部 (b) でいう minibrains とは、ミツバチの場合、具体的にはどのような意味で用いられているか。本文に即して日本語で説明しなさい。

3 下線部 (c) を和訳しなさい。

大学入試

レベル別

英語長文問題 Solution

ソリューション

最新テーマ編

3

トップレベル

スタディサプリ
英語講師
肘井 学
Gaku Hijii

かんき出版

はじめに

“**新時代の英語長文集を作ること**”、このテーマで『大学入試　レベル別英語長文問題ソリューション1～3』を執筆させていただきました。**「解いて終わり」の英語長文はもう終わり**にして、**「出てきた単語を必ず覚える、そして音読を10回することで、1文1文を自分のものにして先に進む」コンセプト**は、たくさんの賛同をいただき、多くの教育者の方々に推奨していただけるほどになりました。

本書は、前作の「**音読がしやすい語数**」という最大の特長を維持しつつ、その語数を音読可能な500語台にまで広げて、**最新のテーマを扱う**という趣旨の英語長文問題集です。**食品廃棄問題、AI、自動運転車、海洋汚染、菜食主義、プラスチックごみ、遠隔教育など、最新のトレンドを扱っています。**ここから本番の試験問題が出題される可能性は非常に高いと言っても差し支えないでしょう。

もっとも、入試本番で、本書で扱ったものと同じテーマや同じ文章が出ても、決して油断しないようにしてください。知っている題材や読み込んだ文章が試験に出題されることは大きなアドバンテージになりますが、あくまで**試験当日に見た文章から客観的に読み取り、その情報から答えを推論すること**、これだけは忘れないでください。

長文中に出てきた単語を必ず覚えること、そして**音読を10回すること**は、**魔法のような相乗効果**をもたらしてくれます。さあ、さっそく本書でも音読のパワーを最大限に味わってください！　**皆さんが信じるべきは、毎日の己の地道な努力であること**を、お忘れないように。

肘井　学

目　次

背景知識が広がるコラム

BACKGROUND KNOWLEDGE

本シリーズの特長

特長その❶　4種類のポイントで万全の英語力が身に付く！

本書では、一文一文の理解に役立つ 構文 POINT 、文と文のつながりを見抜く 論理 POINT 、問題の解き方がわかる 解法 POINT 、語彙(ごい)の本質に強くなる 語彙 POINT と、4種類の**POINT**で体系化して、あらゆる角度から英語力を向上させていきます（p.8〜p.9参照）。

特長その❷　文構造がひと目でわかる構文図解付き！

構文図解で、SVOCMの記号を使って、解釈の手助けをします。必要に応じて、▲マークで**細かい文法事項のメモを入れており、独学でも疑問を残しません**。これと全訳を照らし合わせて、問題を解き終わった後に、**一文一文丁寧に構文把握**をします。

特長その❸　音読用白文・リスニング強化の音声ダウンロード付き！

音読用の白文を掲載しています。**音声ダウンロード**を利用して、音声の後に英文の音読を続けて、**リスニング強化・正確な発音習得**にも役立ててください。問題を解く ⇒ 解説を読む ⇒ 構文把握する ⇒ 単語を覚えた後の**音読10回を必ず行ってください**。

特長その❹　単語帳代わりになる語彙リスト付き！

本書では、本文訳の下に**語彙リスト**を掲載しています。必ず、**出てきた単語をその場で覚えて**ください。

特長その❺　背景知識が広がるコラム付き！

すべての英文に、背景知識が広がるコラムを設けました。背景知識としてあると、**英文を読むのが非常に楽になる**ものを、コラムで紹介しています。自由英作文にはもちろん、他科目にも有効な一生モノの知識が詰まっています。

特長その❻ 最新のテーマを厳選！

時代を反映した最新の頻出テーマである「**食品廃棄問題**」・「**人工知能**」・「**海洋汚染**」・「**菜食主義**」・「**プラスチックごみ問題**」・「**孤独問題**」など、長文の題材を厳選しました。将来の教養として、興味深い題材がそろっています。

特長その❼ 国公立・私立と文系・理系のバランスのとれた題材！

志望大学に左右されない確かな英語力を養うために、出典を**国公立大学と私立大学からバランスよく**選びました。トップレベルなので、出典は早稲田大、慶應大、上智大と旧帝大が中心です。同時に、**文系と理系の両方に精通できる**ような内容を、バランスよく配置しています。

特長その❽ マーク式・記述式の豊富な問題形式・良問揃いの構成！

どの形式でも対応できる英語力を付けるために、**マーク式と記述式の問題をバランスよく配置**しました。さらに、実際の入試問題から、**悪問や奇問を外して、良問をそろえました。**

特長その❾ 音読が可能な300語～500語前後の英文を厳選！

本書で推奨する**音読10回**をやり遂げるために、**音読が可能な300語～500語前後の英文をそろえました。**前作で好評を博した300語前後の文章に加えて、500語前後の文章も扱うことで、より幅広いテーマの英文を扱うことを可能にしました。

4種類のPOINT

構文 POINT

論理 POINT

解法 POINT

語彙 POINT

本シリーズの使い方

❶ 問題を解く

各問題には、制限時間を設けています。それを参考に、**1題20分～30分程度**で、本番を想定して問題を解きます。

⬇

❷ 解答・解説を見て答え合わせをする

悪問・奇問の類は外しています。**4種類のポイント**を中心に解説を読み進めてください。**解答の根拠となる部分は太字で示しています。**

⬇

❸ 英文全体の構文把握や意味を理解する

構文図解と全訳を参考にして、全文を理解します。**主語と動詞の把握、修飾語のカタマリと役割を把握**して、**全文の構文**を確認していきます。

⬇

❹ 知らない単語を必ず覚える

語彙リストを利用して、**英語・日本語セットで3回書いて、10回唱えてください。**単語学習のコツは、何度も繰り返すことです。

⬇

❺ 音声を聞きながら、後に続けて音読を10回する

音声を右ページを参考にダウンロードして、**音声に合わせて、テキストを見ながら10回音読**をします。**句や節といった意味の切れ目を意識して音読**してください。10回目に近付くにつれて、**英語を英語のまま理解できるいわゆる英語脳に近付く**ことができます。**③と④の工程をしっかりやることが**、**スムーズに音読できる最大のコツ**であることを覚えておいてください。

本シリーズのレベル設定

本シリーズは、現状の学力に見合った学習を促すために、下記の表のように、細かいレベル分けをしています。

スタンダードレベル	**日本大、東洋大、駒沢大、専修大**や、**京都産業大、近畿大、甲南大、龍谷大などに代表される私立大学**を目指す人、**共通テストでの平均点以上**や**地方国公立大**を目指す人。
ハイレベル	**学習院大、明治大、青山学院大、立教大、中央大、法政大**や、**関西大、関西学院大、同志社大、立命館大などの難関私大**を目指す人。**共通テストでの高得点や上位国公立大**を目指す人。
トップレベル	**早稲田大、慶応大、上智大、東京理科大**などの**最難関私大**を目指す人。**共通テストで満点**や、**北大、東北大、東京大、名古屋大、京都大、大阪大、九州大などの難関国公立大**を目指す人。

難易度のレベルには変動があり、あくまでも目安です。

音声ダウンロードの方法

No. 01 ヘッドフォンマークの中の番号は音声ファイル内のトラック番号です。

パソコンかスマートフォンで、
右のQRコードを読み取るか

https://kanki-pub.co.jp/pages/ghsaishint/

にアクセスして、音声ファイルをダウンロードしてください。

※音声ダウンロードについてのお問合せ先：https://kanki-pub.co.jp/pages/infodl/

本編に入る前に

● 句と節について

句と節とは、両方とも**意味のカタマリ**と思っていただいて大丈夫です。例えば、When he woke up, the class was over. では、When he woke up までが1つの意味のカタマリで、そこにhe woke upという**SVの文構造があると、節**といいます。かつWhen he woke upはwasを修飾する副詞の働きをしているので、**副詞節**といいます。

また、I like to read comics. という文では、to read comicsが「漫画を読むこと」という意味のカタマリを作っており、そこに**SVがないので、句**といいます。かつto read comicsは「漫画を読むこと」という名詞のカタマリなので、**名詞句**といいます。

節は、**名詞節・形容詞節・副詞節**、句は**名詞句・形容詞句・副詞句**と、意味のカタマリで分類すると、6種類あります。

● カッコについて

名詞のカタマリ（名詞句・名詞節）は〈　　〉で表します。**形容詞のカタマリ（形容詞句・形容詞節）**は（　　）で表し、前の名詞を修飾します。**副詞のカタマリ（副詞句・副詞節）**は[　　]で表し、動詞を修飾します。

● 文の要素について

英文の各パーツを理解するために、**S（主語）**、**V（動詞）**、**O（目的語）**、**C（補語）**、**M（修飾語）**という5つの要素に振り分けます。無理にこの5つに当てはめないほうがいい場合は、何も記号を振りません。

Sは、I go to school. のIのような**日本語の「～は・が」に当たる部分**です。**V**は、goのような**日本語の「～する」に当たる部分**です。**O**はI like soccer. のsoccerのような**動詞の目的語**です。**C**は、I am a teacher. のa teacherのように、**主語やときに目的語の補足説明**をする部分です。

● 品詞について

名詞・形容詞・副詞・前置詞が役割をおさえるべき主要な品詞です。**名詞**は、I like soccer.のように、Iという名詞が**文のS**になったり、soccerという名詞が**文のO**になったり、I am a teacher.のa teacherのように**C**になります。**名詞は文のS・O・C**のいずれかになります。

形容詞は、a cute girlのcuteのように**名詞を修飾**するか、He is old.のoldのように**補語**になります。**形容詞は、名詞を修飾するか文の補語になる**かのいずれかです。

副詞は、very goodのveryのように、うしろの**副詞や形容詞を修飾**します。You can see the world clearly.のclearlyのように「はっきりと見える」と**動詞を修飾**したり、Clearly, you need to exercise.のClearlyのように「明らかに、あなたは運動する必要がある」と、**文を修飾**したりします。**副詞は名詞以外の形容詞・副詞・動詞・文を修飾**します。

前置詞は、The train for Osaka will arrive at nine.のforのように、for Osaka「大阪行きの」という**形容詞のカタマリを作って前の名詞The trainを修飾**したり、atのようにat nine「9時に」という**副詞のカタマリを作って動詞arriveを修飾**したりします。**前置詞は形容詞のカタマリと副詞のカタマリ**を作ります。

● 具体と抽象について

抽象とは、簡単に言うと、**まとめ・まとまり**のことです。それを**具体例**を用いて、わかりやすく説明していくのが、英語に最もよく見られる論理展開です。例えば、
「彼は、**複数の言語**を話すことができる」
「例えば、**日本語・英語・中国語**など」
上の例では、「**(彼の話すことのできる)複数の言語**」が**抽象表現**に当たり、「**日本語・英語・中国語**」が**具体例**です。このつながりが見えてくると、英語長文の理解がグンと深まります。

● 因果関係について

因果関係とは、**原因と結果の関係**のことです。英語の世界では、**こういった原因から、この結果が生まれたという因果関係をとても重視**します。例えば、「昨日とても夜遅くに寝た」という原因から、「今日はとても眠い」という結果が生まれます。

● パラフレーズについて

本書では**パラフレーズ(言い換え)**という用語を多用しています。本来は、phrase「句」という一定の意味のカタマリの言い換えに使いますが、本書では**単語の言い換え、文の言い換えにまで幅広くパラフレーズという用語を使っている**ので、ご承知おきください。

● 関係詞について

関係代名詞(which, who, that, what)と**関係副詞**(when, where, why, how)があります。基本は、**形容詞のカタマリを作って前の名詞を説明する働き**です。例えば、
This is the book **which** I like the best.
「これは私がいちばん好きな本です」
のように、the book に which 以下が説明を加えます。

● 不定詞について

to ＋ **動詞の原形** **を不定詞**といいます。S・O・Cで使う**名詞的用法「～すること」**、名詞を修飾する**形容詞的用法「～する（ための）」**、動詞を修飾する**副詞的用法「～するために」**があります。例えば、
I want something hot **to drink**.「温かい飲み物がほしい」
の**to drink**が**不定詞の形容詞的用法**で、something hot「温かいもの」を修飾しています。

● 分詞と分詞構文について

分詞には、**現在分詞**（doing）と**過去分詞**（done）があります。**形容詞として使用**すると、the window **broken** by the boy「その少年が割った窓」のように、**名詞の後ろにおいて説明を加えます。**

一方で、**分詞を副詞として使用**すると、**分詞構文**になります。全部で3パターンあり、① Doing（Done）～, SV.、② S, doing（done）～, V.、③ SV ～, doing（done）….です。例えば、
Seeing his parents, he ran away.
「両親を見ると、彼は逃げ去った」
のSeeing ～が分詞構文で、「～すると」と接続詞の意味を補って訳します。

問題 1

環 境

人間や他の生物が生態系に与える影響

別冊 p.2 ／制限時間 25 分／ 419 words

解答

Q1. **すべての生き物は、多かれ少なかれ、その物理的環境と、そして生き物同士と、絶えず相互作用している。**

Q2. **象や他の草食動物は1つの平原に影響を与えたが、象よりはるかに小さい光合成細菌が今の大気を作り上げたように、生物の生態系に与える影響は、その大きさに比例するわけではないこと。**

Q3. (ⅰ) **A**　(ⅱ) **D**　(ⅲ) **C**　(ⅳ) **D**

Q4. **A**　**Q5.** **C**

解説

Q1.

下線部(1)を日本語に訳しなさい。
全体の文構造は以下の通りになる。

構文図解

All organisms (S), [to greater or lesser degrees] (M), interact (V) continuously (M) [with their physical environment] (M) and [with each other] (M).

with their physical environment と with each other の接続

All organisms が S で、to ～ degrees が M で、V の interact を修飾する。**to ～ degree** で「**～の程度で**」の意味で、**greater or lesser** が～に入るので、「**多かれ少なかれ**」と訳す。**interact with**「**～と相互作用する**」の interact と with の間に **continuously**「**絶えず**」が入っているので、「～と絶えず相互作用する」と訳す。and が interact with ～の with their physical environment と with each other を接続している。まとめると、「**すべての生き物は、多かれ少なかれ、その物理的環境と、**

そして生き物同士と、絶えず相互作用している」と訳す。

Q2.

この文章の第1段落によると、「象や他の草食動物」や「光合成細菌」のその環境への影響は、「不均衡である」かもしれない。この文脈での「不均衡な影響」とは何を意味するか。日本語で説明しなさい。

解法 POINT ❶ 内容説明問題の解法

内容説明問題の解法は、**該当箇所の抽象的な表現を具体化して**解答します。まずは、**抽象表現がどこかを把握し**、次に**その箇所を具体化**します。

本問では、まず「影響」とは**何が何に与える影響か**がわからないので、抽象表現ととらえる。何が何に与える影響かを明らかにすれば、具体化したことになるので、本文から該当箇所を探す。すると、**第1段落第3文 In some cases, their impact on ecosystems may be disproportionate to their size**.「**その生態系への影響は、その大きさに不均衡な場合もあるかもしれない**」から、theirは前文のAll organismsを指すので、「**生き物**」が「**生態系**」に与える影響とわかる。

続いて、「**不均衡**」とは、**何に対してバランスが取れないかがわからない**ので、抽象表現となる。先ほどと同じ文に**to their size**「**大きさに対して**」とあるので、ここで具体化できることがわかる。実際に後続の文で、**象や他の草食動物は1つの平原に影響を与えた**が、象より**はるかに小さい光合成細菌は今の大気を作り上げた**のだから、**その影響が生物の大きさと比例するわけではない**ことがわかる。以上をまとめると、「**象や他の草食動物は1つの平原に影響を与えたが、象よりはるかに小さい光合成細菌が今の大気を作り上げたように、生物の生態系に与える影響は、その大きさに比例するわけではないこと**」が正解となる。

Q3.

下線(ⅰ)~(ⅳ)の語やフレーズの最も適切な意味を選びなさい。

(ⅰ) 偶然ではなく

A. その結果　B. 偶然　C. でたらめに　D. 予想外に

not coincidentallyは直訳すると「**偶然ではなく**」となる。**B. by**

chance「**偶然**」、C **randomly**「**でたらめに**」は反対の意味なので、正解の候補から外す。Dのunexpectedly「予想外に」は「偶然」と近い意味で、反対になるので不適。消去法で**A. as a result**が正解。文脈を追うと、下線(ⅰ)の語句が含まれている文は ~ , photosynthetic bacteria created the earliest form of the atmosphere as we know it — and, **not coincidentally**, sparked the first Ice Age.「光合成細菌は、私たちが知っている大気の最も古い形態を作り上げ、そして、**結果的に**最初の氷河時代の引き金となった」で、これと合致するので、Aが正解。この文のasに着目する。

構文 POINT ❶ 名詞限定のas

名詞限定のasは、asの接続詞の用法でも、最も難易度が高いので、ここで紹介します。例文をご覧ください。

(例文)

Language **as** we know it is a human invention.

訳 私たちが知っているような言語は、人間が作り出したものだ。

asから意味のカタマリが始まり、itまでの意味のカタマリを作って、Languageを説明しています。itはLanguageを指して、「**私たちが知っているような言語**」と訳します。

名詞限定のasは、knowやunderstandなどの動詞と、説明する名詞の代名詞のitが使われるのが特徴です。

本文では、**the atmosphere as we know it**「**私たちが知っている大気**」で、**名詞限定のas**が使われている。

(ⅱ) (土地を) 不毛にした

A. 削除した　B. 改良した　C. 増やした　D. 弱らせた

下線(ⅱ)の**impoverish**はpoorが隠れているのに気づくと、**imは動詞を作る接頭辞**なので、「**貧しい状態にする**」が原義とわかる。**土地についての説明で使われる**と、「**不毛にする**」、「**やせた状態にする**」となる。よって、**D. weakened**が正解となる。

(ⅲ) 重要な

A. 傲慢(ごうまん)な　B. 調和のとれた　C. 重要な　D. 重大でない

会話表現の**in my not so humble opinion**を紹介する。

語彙 POINT ❶ in my not so humble opinion

会話表現に、**in my not so humble opinion**「**私のそんなに控えめではない意見ですが**」＝「**私の率直な意見ですが**」があります。**to be frank with you**「**率直に言うと**」はストレートな言い回しで、それよりもやや柔らかい印象を与える表現です。

本問でも、**not-so-humble**「**そんなに控えめではない**」＝「**重要な**」となる。B. harmoniousやD. minorは反対の意味になるので不適。A. arrogantは言い過ぎなので不適。消去法で**C. key**が正解となる。文脈でも、**人間以外が生態系に重要な影響を与える具体例が列挙されている**ので、Cが正解と特定できる。

（iv） ～と同等で

A. ～と異なって　　B. ～に傷害を負わされて

C. ～以下で　　D. ～と似て

下線（iv）を含んだ英文は、主語がhumans、目的語がmany other organismsなので、**環境への影響の点で、人間と他の生き物を本文ではどうとらえているか**に着目する。**第3段落第1文**で、「**人間だけが環境に大きな影響を与えているわけではない**」という趣旨の文があり、それ以降で**その他に環境に影響を与えている生き物の具体例が列挙**されているので、**D. similar to**が正解とわかる。ちなみに、**par**は「**同等**」の意味なので、**on a par with**「**～と同等で**」となる。

Q4.

次の(A, B, C, D)のうち、この文章の最終段落を最もよく要約したものはどれか。

A. 人間は自然に対して限定的な支配力を持つ。

B. 人間は自然と協調しなければならない。

C. 人間は自然環境をコントロールする方法を選ばなければならない。

D. 人間は自然を破壊し続けるだろう。

最終段落最終文Nature, much like human society, typically declines to follow the scripts we sometimes choose to write for it.「**自然は**、人間社会とほぼ同様に、**私たちが時にそのために書くと決**

めた原稿通りに進むことを、たいていは拒むのだ」から、**A Humans have limited control over nature.** が正解。本文の「**自然は人間の思い通りにならない**」を、Aで「**自然に対して限定的な支配力を持つ**」と言い換えている。他の選択肢は本文に記述なし。

Q5.

最終段落には、自然へのマイナスの影響を説明するのに下線部(2)環境被害がある。次の(A, B, C, D)のうち、この文章の「環境被害」の例として使用されていないのはどれか。

A. 空気組成の変化　　B. 動物の絶滅
C. 土壌の生産　　　　D. 水質の変化

NOT問題は消去法で解答する。**下線部(2)のenvironmental traumaは、第2段落第1文のenvironmental damageと同義**なので、この段落に複数の環境被害が列挙されていることに気付く。**第2段落第2文**の**have generated large volumes of certain gasesがA. air composition changeに該当**する。同文の**altered the acidity of riversがD. water quality changeに該当**するので、ともに正解の候補から外す。

同段落第3文Surprising numbers of species have been driven to extinction as human populations have grown worldwide.「驚くほど多数の種が、人口が世界中で増加するにつれて、絶滅に追いやられた」は、B. animal extinctionに該当するとわかるので、正解の候補から外す。

よって、残った**C. soil productionが環境被害の例ではない**ので正解となる。**soil production**は、第3段落第2～4文で、**人間以外の動物が、自分たちが生息するための土壌を形成した**とあるので、環境被害の例には当たらないとわかる。

構文図解

Ecological systems are the products (of the organisms) (that inhabit them). All organisms, [to greater or lesser degrees], interact continuously [with their physical environment] and [with each other]. [In some cases], their impact (on ecosystems) may be disproportionate [to their size]. Elephants and other grazing animals have made the Serengeti plains 〈what they are〉, [from the characteristics of the grasses on which they tread to the chemical structure of the soil]. [Billions of years ago], photosynthetic bacteria created the earliest form (of the atmosphere as we know it) — and, [not coincidentally], sparked the first Ice Age. All organisms have a constant and never-ending impact on their ecosystems.

S: Ecological systems / V: are / C: the products / M: (of the organisms) (that inhabit them)
関係代名詞: that
them: ecological systemsを指す
S: All organisms / M: to greater or lesser degrees / V: interact / M: continuously / M: with their physical environment / M: with each other
M: In some cases / S: their impact / M: on ecosystems / V: may be / C: disproportionate / M: to their size
S: Elephants and other grazing animals / V: have made / O: the Serengeti plains / C: what they are / M: from the characteristics ... to the chemical structure of the soil
関係代名詞: what
they: the Serengeti plainsを指す
they: elephants and other grazing animalsを指す
to: from A to B「AからBまで」のto
M: Billions of years ago / S: photosynthetic bacteria / V: created / O: the earliest form / M: of the atmosphere as we know it
名詞限定のas「〜ような」
it: the atmosphereを指す
M: not coincidentally / V: sparked / O: the first Ice Age
S: All organisms / V: have a constant and never-ending impact on / O: their ecosystems

[In the long span of human history], the vast majority (of environmental damage) has occurred [in only the past three centuries]. [Fueled by industrialization and modernization], humans have generated (large volumes of) certain gases, altered the acidity (of rivers), used up underground water sources, introduced alien species, and impoverished landscapes [as they extract and consume resources]. (Surprising numbers of) species have been driven [to extinction] [as human populations have grown worldwide].

M: In the long span of human history / S: the vast majority / M: of environmental damage / V: has occurred / M: in only the past three centuries
M: Fueled by industrialization and modernization / S: humans / V: have generated / M: large volumes of / O: certain gases / V: altered / O: the acidity / M: of rivers / V: used up / O: underground water sources / V: introduced / O: alien species / V: impoverished / O: landscapes / M: as they extract and consume resources
分詞構文: Fueled
5つのhave p.p.のp.p.の接続: and
they: humansを指す
M: Surprising numbers of / S: species / V: have been driven / M: to extinction / M: as human populations have grown worldwide
時のas

本文訳

生態系システムは、そこに生息する生き物の産物だ。すべての生き物は、多かれ少なかれ、その物理的環境と、そして生き物同士と、絶えず相互作用している。その生態系への影響は、その大きさに不均衡な場合もあるかもしれない。象や他の草食動物は、彼らが踏みつける草の特徴から土壌の化学構造まで、*セレンゲティ平原を今の状態にした。何十億年前、光合成細菌が、私たちが知っている大気の最も古い形態を作り上げ、そして、結果的に、最初の氷河時代の引き金となったのは偶然ではない。あらゆる生き物が、その生態系に絶えず、決して終わることのない影響を与えている。

人類史の長い期間で、環境被害の圧倒的大多数が、このわずか3世紀の間で起きた。工業化や近代化にあおられて、人間は大量の例のガスを発生させ、川の酸性度を変え、地下水資源を使い果たし、外来種を混入させ、資源を抽出して消費することで、土地を不毛にした。驚くほど多数の種が、人口が世界中で増加するにつれて、絶滅に追いやられた。

*「セレンゲティ平原」は、ライオン、キリンなどの様々な動物が生息するタンザニア北部にある国立公園の平原。

語彙リスト

☐	ecological	形 生態系の
☐	product	名 産物
☐	organism	名 有機体
☐	inhabit	動 ～に住んでいる
☐	to ～ degree	熟 ～の程度で
☐	interact with	熟 ～と相互作用する
☐	disproportionate	形 不釣り合いな
☐	graze	形 草を食べる
☐	plain	名 平野
☐	characteristics	名 特徴
☐	tread on	熟 ～を踏む
☐	photosynthetic bacteria	名 光合成細菌
☐	form	名 形態
☐	atmosphere	名 大気
☐	coincidentally	副 偶然に
☐	spark	動 ～の引き金となる
☐	have an impact on	熟 ～に影響を与える
☐	fuel	動 ～をあおる
☐	generate	動 ～を発生させる
☐	alter	動 変える
☐	acidity	名 酸性度
☐	underground	形 地下の
☐	alien	形 外来の
☐	impoverish	動 不毛にする
☐	landscape	名 地形
☐	extract	動 抽出する
☐	drive A to B	熟 AをBに追いやる
☐	extinction	名 絶滅

▸単語10回CHECK 1 ☐ 2 ☐ 3 ☐ 4 ☐ 5 ☐ 6 ☐ 7 ☐ 8 ☐ 9 ☐ 10 ☐

構文図解

Human activity has clearly had an enormous effect on the natural environment.
S V O

Humans, however, are not unique [in their power to reshape environments locally or globally]. Burrowing rodents, [for example], maintain vast grasslands (rich in their favorite foods) [by continuously turning the soil and discouraging the growth of forests]. Sheep, [brought to Mexico with the European settlement], created their own grazing land [through the action of their hooves on the soil]. Then there are the not-so-humble roles (of microbes, worms, and other invertebrates) [in soil formation and rejuvenation]. Some plant species have redefined the conditions (of natural selection for countless living things and geological processes alike). The lesson is 〈that humans, in their effects on the environment, are on a par with many other organisms〉.

S M V C M (to: 不定詞 形容詞的用法) / S M / V O (rich: 形容詞の後置修飾) M / M / S (brought: 分詞構文) M V / O M / M M V S M (and: microbes, worms, other invertebratesの接続) M / S V O M / S V / (that: 名詞節のthat) C

The key (to comprehending environmental history) is an understanding (of the bonds that have formed between humans and other species), for these have generated co-evolutionary processes [with their own logic and drive]. [In many ecosystems today], humans are the dominant species. But such dominance cannot exist [apart from the systems and processes that sustain it].

S M V C (that: 関係代名詞) O / (for: 接続詞のfor「というのは～だから」) (these: the bondsを指す) S V O / M M / S V C / (such dominance: 現代の生態系の中で人間が支配的な種であること) S V / M (that: 関係代名詞) (it: such dominanceを指す)

本文訳

人間の活動が、自然環境に非常に多くの影響を与えてきたのは明らかだ。

しかし、人間は*局地的に、あるいは世界的規模で環境を作り変える力を持った唯一の存在ではない。例えば、*穴居性(けっきょせい)げっ歯類(しるい)は、絶えず土壌を掘り起こして森林の*繁茂(はんも)を抑えることで、大好物の食べ物が豊富な広大な牧草地を維持している。羊は、ヨーロッパ人の入植に伴ってメキシコに連れてこられたが、土壌を踏みつけることで、自分たちの牧草地を作った。そして、土壌の形成や活性化において、微生物、虫、他の*無脊椎(むせきつい)動物が、重要な役割を果たしている。無数の生き物と地質作用の双方を同様に、自然淘汰の条件と再定義する元となった植物種もある。教訓として、人間は、環境へのその影響の点で、他の多くの生き物と同等なのである。

環境史を理解するのに重要なのは、人間と他の種の間に発生した結び付きを理解することである。というのは、これらの結び付きが、それ自体の論理と推進力でともに進化する過程を生み出してきたからだ。現代では多くの生態系で、人間は優占種だ。しかし、そのような優位性は、それを維持するシステムや過程と離れて存在することはできない。

*「局地的に」は、物事や現象がある地域に限られているさま。
*「穴居性げっ歯類」は、穴の中にすみ、地上で食物をとるネズミのような生き物。
*「繁茂」は、草木が生い茂ること。
*「無脊椎動物」は、クラゲやナメクジのように脊椎を持たない動物。

語彙リスト

have an effect on	熟	～に影響を与える
enormous	形	巨大な
reshape	動	作り変える
burrow	動	穴に住む
rodent	名	げっ歯類
discourage	動	妨げる
settlement	名	入植
hooves (hoofの複数形)	名	(馬や牛などの)ひづめ
humble	形	慎ましい
microbe	名	微生物
worm	名	虫
invertebrate	名	無脊椎動物
rejuvenation	名	活性化
redefine	動	再定義する
natural selection	名	自然淘汰
geological	形	地質の
on a par with	熟	～と同等で
comprehend	動	理解する
bond	名	結び付き
evolutionary	形	進化の
drive	名	推進力
dominant	形	支配的な
apart from	熟	～と離れて
sustain	動	維持する

▸単語10回CHECK 1 2 3 4 5 6 7 8 9 10

構文図解

The effects (of environmental trauma) are real, but they are a product (of scale), not human exceptionalism. [Although the human impact on the planet today is surely the result of human actions and behavior], this should never be confused [with intention or control]. Nature, [much like human society], typically declines ⟨to follow the scripts we sometimes choose to write for it⟩.

The effects: S / (of environmental trauma): M / are: V / real: C / they: S（the effectsを指す） / are: V / a product: C / (of scale): M / not human exceptionalism: M（B, not A「AではなくB」） / [Although the human impact on the planet today is surely the result of human actions and behavior]: M / this: S（人間の地球への影響が人間の行動の結果であること） / should never be confused: V / [with intention or control]: M / Nature: S / [much like human society]: M（前置詞のlike） / typically: M / declines: V / ⟨to follow the scripts we sometimes choose to write for it⟩: O（to: 不定詞 名詞的用法 / scripts we: 関係代名詞の省略 / it: natureを指す）

本文訳

環境被害の影響は実際にあるが、それらは *人間例外主義ではなくて、*規模の産物だ。現代の人間の地球への影響は、確実に人間の活動やふるまいの結果だが、このことを意図や支配と混同すべきではない。自然は、人間社会とほぼ同様に、私たちが時にそのために書くと決めた原稿通りに進むことを、たいていは拒むのだ。

*human exceptionalism「人間例外主義」とは、人間が他の動物とは異なる存在で、優れているという考え方のこと。

*a product of scale「規模の産物」とは、人間の活動規模が大きくなった結果、産み出したものという意味で使われている。

語彙リスト

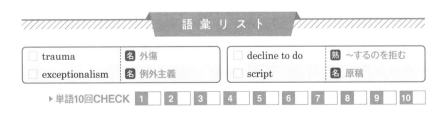

trauma	名	外傷
exceptionalism	名	例外主義
decline to do	熟	～するのを拒む
script	名	原稿

▸単語10回CHECK 1 2 3 4 5 6 7 8 9 10

Ecological systems are the products of the organisms that inhabit them. All organisms, to greater or lesser degrees, interact continuously with their physical environment and with each other. In some cases, their impact on ecosystems may be disproportionate to their size. Elephants and other grazing animals have made the Serengeti plains what they are, from the characteristics of the grasses on which they tread to the chemical structure of the soil. Billions of years ago, photosynthetic bacteria created the earliest form of the atmosphere as we know it — and, not coincidentally, sparked the first Ice Age. All organisms have a constant and never-ending impact on their ecosystems.

In the long span of human history, the vast majority of environmental damage has occurred in only the past three centuries. Fueled by industrialization and modernization, humans have generated large volumes of certain gases, altered the acidity of rivers, used up underground water sources, introduced alien species, and impoverished landscapes as they extract and consume resources. Surprising numbers of species have been driven to extinction as human populations have grown worldwide. Human activity has clearly had an enormous effect on the natural environment.

Humans, however, are not unique in their power to reshape environments locally or globally. Burrowing rodents, for example, maintain vast grasslands rich in their favorite foods by continuously turning the soil and discouraging the growth of forests. Sheep, brought to Mexico with the European settlement, created their own grazing land through the action of their hooves on the soil. Then there are the not-so-humble roles of microbes, worms, and other invertebrates in soil formation and rejuvenation. Some plant species have redefined the conditions of natural selection for countless living things and geological processes alike. The lesson is that humans, in their effects on the environment, are on a par with many other organisms.

The key to comprehending environmental history is an

understanding of the bonds that have formed between humans and other species, for these have generated co-evolutionary processes with their own logic and drive. In many ecosystems today, humans are the dominant species. But such dominance cannot exist apart from the systems and processes that sustain it. The effects of environmental trauma are real, but they are a product of scale, not human exceptionalism. Although the human impact on the planet today is surely the result of human actions and behavior, this should never be confused with intention or control. Nature, much like human society, typically declines to follow the scripts we sometimes choose to write for it.

▶音読10回CHECK 1 2 3 4 5 6 7 8 9 10

背景知識が広がるコラム

BACKGROUND KNOWLEDGE

生物多様性の喪失の要因

人間が環境に与える影響は無数にありますが、その中でも近年注目されているのが、本文にあったように、**大量絶滅を含む生物多様性の喪失**です。

では、**生物多様性の喪失の間接的・直接的要因**となっている問題は、具体的に何でしょうか。まずは**人口爆発**が挙げられます。世界の人口は18世紀以降に爆発的に増加しており、**人口過多が、生物圏全体に対する最大の脅威**と見なす考え方もあるようです。そして、**人口爆発に伴って、地球環境を悪化させている**のが**資源の過剰消費**です。過剰消費の一例として、**畜産業**が挙げられます。

畜産業とは、**家畜・家禽(かきん)を飼育して、乳製品、肉、卵、皮革などの畜産物を得て生活に役立てる産業のこと**を言います。家禽とは、卵を産んでくれるニワトリを想像するとわかりやすいでしょう。私たちが普通に享受している**肉食**は、実は**環境に多大なダメージ**を与えているのです。

具体的には、まず家畜の飼料となる植物の栽培に使われる、**水の大量消費**です。次に、**家畜の放牧にあてられる土地資源の利用**です。広大な牧場を想像してもらえればわかるでしょう。放牧のために**森林伐採**が行われ、森林消失によって生息地を失った**種の絶滅**などの悪影響があります。一部の研究によると、**畜産業こそが、森林伐採と生息地破壊の大きな要因**であり、**生物多様性の喪失の一因**となっているそうです。

畜産業だけではありません。**農業**も、**大きな環境被害**をもたらしています。田んぼのある広大な風景を想像してくれればわかるでしょう。地球上の土地の大部分が農業に使われているので、**農地の使用により植物種が絶滅へと追いやられて、農業も生物多様性の喪失の一因**とされています。農業で使用される**農薬**も、環境へ大きなダメージを与えています。**散布された殺虫剤、除草剤などが、生物種、空気、水、土地を汚染**していきます。

畜産業、農業に加えて、漁業も環境へ多大なダメージを与えています。**サンゴ礁などの生息地破壊**のみならず、**乱獲により、やはり生物多様性の喪失**につながっていきます。

改めて、**私たちが日々口にするものへの感謝、そして有難さを認識しながら、食べ物を大事にすることを実践していかなければなりません。**

問題 **2**

生物

動物のコミュニケーション

別冊 p.6 ／制限時間 25 分／ 490 words

解答

1. ③ 2. ④ 3. ① 4. ② 5. ④
6. ④ 7. ③ 8. ②

解説

1.

① 勝る ② 傾向がある ③ 得意な ④ しがちである

aptについては、**be apt to do「～する傾向にある」**を、まずはおさえる。「**～する傾向にある**」のパラフレーズの問題は頻出なので、以下に整理する。

語彙 POINT ❷ 「～する傾向にある」のパラフレーズ

tend to do ／ be inclined to do ／ be apt to do ／ be prone to do ／ be liable to do

「**～する傾向にある**」は、**tend to doが一番一般的な表現**で、続いて、**be inclined to do**は、**人の性格やその物の性質上何かをする傾向にあるとき**に使います。**be apt to do, be prone to do, be liable to do**は、**あまりよくないことをする傾向にあるとき**に使います。**apt**や**liable**は「**～しそうだ**」という意味では、**be likely to do**とも同義になり、このパラフレーズも頻出です。

本問は、be apt atなので、上記のパラフレーズをおさえておけば、② proneと④ liableは用法が異なるので不適とわかる。**be apt at**は**be good at「～が得意だ」**と**同じ形**で、文脈上も意味が通るので③が正解。

2.

① もし～なら ② ～しない限り ③ ～でさえ ④ 一方で

空所 [2] を含む文は、In **terrestrial mammals**, the structure of the utterances is generally considered to be **innate**, [2] **songbirds** have to **learn** (based on innate biases) their species-specific songs. で、**terrestrial mammals**「**陸生の哺乳動物**」と **songbirds**「**鳴き鳥**」、**innate**「**先天的な**」と **learn**「**(後天的に) 学ぶ**」から対比構造だと気づけば、④ whileが正解とわかる。「**先天的**」、「**後天的**」の対比構造は頻出なので、以下に整理する。

論理 POINT ❶ 「先天的」・「後天的」の対比

●「先天的な」を意味する語
innate / inherent / natural / inborn / hereditary
●「後天的な」を意味する語
acquired / learned

「**先天的な**」とは「生まれつき身に付いていること」を意味し、**innate / inherent / natural / inborn** などがあります。**hereditary**は「**遺伝上の**」で、やはり**生まれつき備わっていること**を意味します。「**後天的な**」とは「生まれてから身に付けたこと」を意味し、**acquired, learned** などがあるので、おさえておきましょう。

3.

① 概して　② 対照的に　③ 当然ながら　④ 今度だけは

空所の後ろの**typical**「**典型的な**」に着目すると**一般論を表している**のがわかるので、① **Altogether**「**概して**」(**=一般的に**) が正解。

4.

下線部(4)のThe sameは、前文「**組み合わせた信号の数は、その信号を構成する要素よりも、実質的には少ない**」を指す。**信号が歌**を指し、**信号を構成する要素が歌の構成要素**を指すので、② **歌を構成する要素の方が、歌の数よりも多いこと**が正解。

5.

① ～より多い　② ～も　③ わずか　④ ～より少ない

空所 [5] を含む文は、The same appears to be true for humpback

whales, and is strikingly different from human language, in which the number of words is orders of magnitude [5] the number of possible sentences.である。まとめると、「**同じこと（信号の数が構成要素の数より少ないこと）が、ザトウクジラにも当てはまるように思えるが、ヒトの言語とは大きく異なり、～**」となる。この文の**and**は**逆接**「**しかし**」を意味することに注意する。

よって、**人の言語では、信号（＝文）が構成要素（＝単語）の数より多い、すなわち、単語の数は文より少なくなる**ので、④ **less than**が正解。

6.

① 複雑な　② 複合的な　③ 洗練された　④ **意義のある**

下線部(6)は**elaborate**「**入念な、手の込んだ**」の意味の単語。① **intricate**、② **complex**はともに「**複雑な**」なので、正解の候補から外れる。③ **sophisticated**は「**洗練された**」に加えて「**精巧な**」、「**複雑な**」の意味もあるので、不適。正解は④「**意義のある**」の**meaningful**。

語彙 POINT ❸ 「複雑な」のパラフレーズ

complicated ／ complex ／ intricate ／ mixed ／ sophisticated ／ elaborate

「**複雑な**」のパラフレーズも頻出なので、確認しておきましょう。**complex**は厳密には「**複合的な**」という意味で、**複数のものが合わさっているイメージ**です。**複合施設**を**コンプレックス**と言いますが、**映画館や本屋、洋服屋などの複数の店が入った建物**です。**mixed**は「**感情などが混ざり合って**」＝「**複雑な**」となります。**sophisticated**や**elaborate**は、同様に「**（ものの作りが）精巧な**」＝「**複雑な**」となります。

7.

下線部(7)は、There is, however, good evidence for the second pointで、the second pointは(b)の「**その配列のおかげで、聞き手が様々な鳴き声の単位の組み合わせに基づいて、意味の差異をとらえているかどうかだ**」を指す。よって、③ **霊長類は鳴き声の組み合わせによって意味を区別している証拠がある**。が正解となる。

8.

① 動物のコミュニケーションは、一般的に記号システムに基づいていると考えられている。

② 様々な動物が、そのコミュニケーションシステムを獲得するのに様々な過程を経ている。

③ 鳥の鳴き声と人間の言語は、両者が組み合わせの方法を活用して、ほぼ無限の信号を作り出すという点で似ている。

④ クジラの鳴き声は、人間だけが別々の単位を組み合わせて1つのフレーズを作ることができるという点で、人間の言語とは異なる。

第1段落第3文 Further analyses of the structure of animal communication need to take into account that **both the acquisition and the performance of vocal behavior differ substantially between different taxa.**「動物のコミュニケーションの構造をさらに分析するには、**発声行動の習得と実践の両方が、分類上、種類が異なるとかなり違う**ことを考慮に入れる必要がある。」から、② **Different animals undergo different processes in acquiring their communication systems.** が**正解**。

不正解の選択肢を見ていくと、①は第1段落第1文**A striking feature of most,** if not all, **animal communication is the lack of a symbolic structure**.「すべてではないにせよ、**ほとんどの動物のコミュニケーションの際立った特徴は、記号的構造がないことだ**」に反するので不適。③は第1段落第10文に反する。**同文は、鳴き鳥と同じこと、すなわち信号の数は構成要素の数より少ないことがザトウクジラには当てはまるがヒトには当てはまらない**という内容。すなわち、人間は無数の組み合わせで無限の信号を作り出せるが、鳥はそうではないので不適。

④は、**第1段落第11文**The most elaborate bird and **whale song exploits two main devices: ~ sequencing of up to about seven separate units (perhaps iterated) into a single phrase**で、クジラと鳥が別々の単位を組み合わせて、1つのフレーズを作ることができるという内容に反するので不適。

構文図解

A striking feature (of most, if not all, animal communication) is
S　M　「すべてではないにせよ」　V

the lack (of a symbolic structure). Most (of the complexity in animal
C　M　S　M

communication) can be explained [by the fact that listeners are apt
V　M　同格のthat

at extracting information from signals, while the sender does not
M

always intend to provide that information]. Further analyses (of the
S

structure of animal communication) need to take [into account] ⟨that
M　V　M　名詞節のthat

both the acquisition and the performance of vocal behavior differ
O（takeの目的語）

substantially between different taxa⟩. [In terrestrial mammals], the
M　S

structure (of the utterances) is generally considered to be innate,
M　V　to be　C

[while songbirds have to learn (based on innate biases) their species-
M

specific songs]. Some animals produce (series of) repetitions (of the
S　V　M　O　M

same sound (e.g., the croaking of a frog)), [whereas others utter
M

strings of different notes, often composed into higher-order
分詞構文

structures]. The structure (of both birdsong and humpback whale
S　M

songs) has been explored. One (of the most elaborate singers among
V　S　M

the songbirds), the nightingale, commands up to 200 song types,
S′　V　O

付帯状況のwith
[with each consisting of a succession of several elements or notes].
with O CのO　with O CのC　M

Altogether, the song (of a typical nightingale) may have up to 1000
M　S　M　V　O

different elements.

本文訳

すべてではないにせよ、ほとんどの動物のコミュニケーションの際立った特徴は、記号的構造がないことだ。動物のコミュニケーションの複雑さのほとんどが、聞く側は信号から情報を引き出すのが得意だが、送る側が必ずしもその情報を提供するつもりであるとは限らないという事実によって説明できる。動物のコミュニケーションの構造をさらに分析するには、発声行動の習得と実践の両方が、分類上、種類が異なるとかなり違うことを考慮に入れる必要がある。陸生の哺乳動物では、発声の構造は、一般的には先天的に備わっていると思われているが、それに対して鳴き鳥は、(先天的な興味に基づいて) その種固有の鳴き声を身につけなければならない。動物の中には、同じ音 (例えばカエルの鳴き声) を連続して繰り返すものもいる。一方で、高次構造へと構成されることが多いが、一連の異なる音を発する動物もいる。鳴き鳥とザトウクジラの鳴き声の両方の構造が探求されてきた。鳴き鳥の中で最も精巧な鳴き声を出す鳥の1つである*ナイチンゲールは、200もの種類の鳴き声を操り、それぞれの鳴き声は複数の要素や音の連続で構成されている。概して、典型的なナイチンゲールの鳴き声には、1000もの異なる要素が含まれていることもある。

*「ナイチンゲール」は、ツグミ類の渡り鳥。別名サヨナキドリ。

語彙リスト

striking	形	際立った
feature	名	特徴
symbolic	形	記号による
structure	名	構造
complexity	名	複雑さ
be apt at	熟	～が得意だ
extract	動	抽出する
sender	名	発信者
analyses	名	analysisの複数形
take O into account	熟	Oを考慮する
acquisition	名	獲得
substantially	副	かなり
taxa (taxonの複数形)	名	分類単位
terrestrial	形	陸生の
mammal	名	哺乳動物
utterance	名	発声
innate	形	先天的な
songbird	名	鳴き鳥
bias	名	興味
-specific	形	～特有の
repetition	名	反復
croak	動	(カエルが)ガーガー鳴く
frog	名	カエル
whereas	接	一方で
utter	動	発する
strings of	熟	一連の～
note	名	音
be composed into	熟	～に組み入れられる
elaborate	形	入念な、精巧な
command	動	自由に操る
succession	名	連続
element	名	要素
altogether	副	概して

▸単語10回CHECK 1 2 3 4 5 6 7 8 9 10

構文図解

Thus, the number (of combinatorial signals) is effectively smaller
M S M V C
[than the elements which make up the signal]. The same appears to
M 信号の数が信号の構成要素より少ないこと S V
be true [for humpback whales], and is strikingly different [from
C M V C M
human language], [in which the number of words is orders of
M
magnitude less than the number of possible sentences]. The most
orders of magnitude 比較級「桁違いに～」 同格のコロン「すなわち」 S
elaborate bird and whale song exploits two main devices: repetition
V O
of syllables or phrases, and sequencing of up to about seven separate
O′ repetition ～ と sequencing ～ の接続
units (perhaps iterated) into a single phrase, itself perhaps iterated.

Most significantly, bird and whale songs are combinatorial but not
M S V C C
semantically compositional [in the sense that the elements that
M 同格のthat 関係代名詞のthat
make up the utterances carry specific meaning].
the elementsに対応するV 比較級の強調「ずっと」C

Perplexingly, the utterances (of nonhuman primates) are much
M S M V
less elaborate [than that of songbirds or whales], [with the notable
C the utteranceを指す M M
exception of gibbon song], [despite the fact that nonhuman primates
同格のthat
do not simply utter signal calls, but rather bouts of several calls].

本文訳

したがって、組み合わせた信号の数は、その信号を構成する要素よりも、実質的には少ない。同じことがザトウクジラにも当てはまるように思えるが、単語の数が考えられる文の数より桁違いに少ないヒトの言語とは著しく異なる。最も精巧な鳥やクジラの鳴き声は、2つの主要な方法を活用している。すなわち、音節やフレーズの繰り返しと、およそ7つまでの別々の単位を（おそらく反復して）1つのフレーズに配列することである。そのフレーズ自体がおそらく反復されている。最も重要なことは、鳥やクジラの鳴き声は組み合わせだが、発声を構成する要素が特別な意味を伝えるという点で、意味を考えて構成されてはいない。

困惑することに、ヒトではない霊長類は、単に信号音を発するだけでなく、むしろ一定時間複数の音を発するという事実にもかかわらず、その発声は、テナガザルの鳴き声という注目すべき例外があるが、鳴き鳥やクジラの鳴き声よりずっと精巧ではない。

語彙リスト

combinatorial	形	組み合わせの
effectively	副	実質的には
make up	熟	構成する
strikingly	副	著しく
order of magnitude	名	桁
exploit	動	～を活用する
device	名	方法
syllable	名	音節
sequencing	名	配列すること
unit	名	単位
semantically	副	意味論的に
compositional	形	構成の
perplexingly	副	困惑することに
primate	名	霊長類
notable	形	注目すべき
exception	名	例外
bout	名	一期間

▸単語10回CHECK 1 2 3 4 5 6 7 8 9 10

構文図解

人間ではない霊長類が単一ではなく連続した鳴き声を上げること

The question is (a) 〈whether such sequences can be described in

S　V　名詞節のwhether「～かどうか」　C

terms of syntactical rules〉, and (b) 〈whether they allow listeners to

such sequencesを指す　C

attribute differential meaning based on the combination of different

call units〉. The first point can be largely refuted [as sequences do not

S　(a)を指す　V　理由のas　M

follow fully predictable patterns]; instead, signal combinations can

M　S　V

be described more appropriately [in probabilistic terms]. There is,

M　M　M　V

however, good evidence [for the second point]. [Since most monkey

M　S　M　(b)を指す　理由のsince　M

and ape species have relatively small repertoires], this constraint

ほとんどのサルや類人猿の種が比較的少ないレパートリーしか持っていないこと　S

may have favored listeners' abilities (to process signal combinations).

V　O　不定詞 形容詞的用法　M

[On the production side], it remains unclear 〈whether the processes

M　形式主語のit S　V　C　S′

that give rise to heterotypic call sequences (i.e., successions of

関係代名詞のthat

関係代名詞のthat

different call types) are fundamentally different from those that lead

the processesを指す

to series of the same call〉.

本文訳

問題は、(a) その音の配列が、文法的な規則の観点で説明できるかどうか、そして(b) その配列のおかげで、聞き手が様々な鳴き声の単位の組み合わせに基づいて、意味の差異をとらえているかどうかだ。最初の点は、配列が完全に予測できるパターンにならっていないので、ほとんど論破することができる。その代わりに、信号の組み合わせは、確率的な点から、もっと適切に説明できる。しかし、第2の点には、しっかりした証拠がある。ほとんどの猿や類人猿の種が比較的少ないレパートリーしか持っていないので、この制約が、信号の組み合わせを処理する聞き手の能力に味方したのかもしれない。音を生み出す側からは、異質な鳴き声の配列（例えば、異なる音の種類の連続）を生じる過程が、一連の鳴き声を生み出す過程とは根本的に異なるかどうかは、依然として明らかではない。

語彙リスト

describe	動 ～を説明する	probabilistic	形 確率的な
in terms of	熟 ～の観点で	ape	名 類人猿
attribute	動 ～を持っているとみなす	repertoire	名 レパートリー
refute	動 論破する	constraint	名 制約
predictable	形 予測できる	give rise to	熟 生じる
in ~ terms	熟 ～の点から	heterotypic	形 異質な

▸単語10回CHECK 1 2 3 4 5 6 7 8 9 10

A striking feature of most, if not all, animal communication is the lack of a symbolic structure. Most of the complexity in animal communication can be explained by the fact that listeners are apt at extracting information from signals, while the sender does not always intend to provide that information. Further analyses of the structure of animal communication need to take into account that both the acquisition and the performance of vocal behavior differ substantially between different taxa. In terrestrial mammals, the structure of the utterances is generally considered to be innate, while songbirds have to learn (based on innate biases) their species-specific songs. Some animals produce series of repetitions of the same sound (e.g., the croaking of a frog) , whereas others utter strings of different notes, often composed into higher-order structures. The structure of both birdsong and humpback whale songs has been explored. One of the most elaborate singers among the songbirds, the nightingale, commands up to 200 song types, with each consisting of a succession of several elements or notes. Altogether, the song of a typical nightingale may have up to 1000 different elements. Thus, the number of combinatorial signals is effectively smaller than the elements which make up the signal. The same appears to be true for humpback whales, and is strikingly different from human language, in which the number of words is orders of magnitude less than the number of possible sentences. The most elaborate bird and whale song exploits two main devices: repetition of syllables or phrases, and sequencing of up to about seven separate units (perhaps iterated) into a single phrase, itself perhaps iterated. Most significantly, bird and whale songs are combinatorial but not semantically compositional in the sense that the elements that make up the utterances carry specific meaning.

Perplexingly, the utterances of nonhuman primates are much less elaborate than that of songbirds or whales, with the notable exception of gibbon song, despite the fact that nonhuman primates do not simply utter signal calls, but rather bouts of several calls. The question is (a) whether such sequences can be described in terms of syntactical rules, and (b) whether they allow listeners to attribute differential meaning based on the combination of different call units. The first point can be largely refuted as sequences do not follow fully predictable patterns; instead, signal combinations can be described more appropriately in probabilistic terms. There is, however, good evidence for the second point. Since most monkey and ape species have relatively small repertoires, this constraint may have favored listeners' abilities to process signal combinations. On the production side, it remains unclear whether the processes that give rise to heterotypic call sequences (i.e., successions of different call types) are fundamentally different from those that lead to series of the same call.

▸音読10回CHECK 1 2 3 4 5 6 7 8 9 10

背景知識が広がるコラム

BACKGROUND KNOWLEDGE

動物の様々なコミュニケーション

近年、動物の高度な認知能力（第10問のコラムで紹介します）や、**動物の様々なコミュニケーション能力**に注目が集まっています。

最も簡単な動物のコミュニケーションの例として、**カニのハサミを振り上げた求愛行動**があります。ハサミを振り上げて「自分は健康体だ」と合図することで、交尾する相手を探します。

次に、大学入試問題の題材にもなった**ミツバチの尻振りダンス**です。**尻振りダンス**とは、**円形ダンスや8の字ダンス**のことで、**働きバチが仲間にエサの場を教えるコミュニケーション**です。

さらに、こちらも多くの論文で取り上げられて、大学入試の題材になっている**クジラの鳴き声**です。**クジラの鳴き声**とは、**コミュニケーションを目的とした、ザトウクジラが発する一連の音**を指します。その音は**反復的でパターンが予測可能な音で、人間の歌を連想させるもの**なので、**クジラの歌**と呼ばれています。

そして、**イルカ**には、**エコーロケーション**と呼ばれる**超音波を使ったコミュニケーション方法**があります。超音波とは振動数16,000ヘルツ以上の音波で、人間の耳では音として感じられないものです。この**超音波**によって、**仲間とエサの位置や大きさ、周囲の地形や状況を意思疎通**することができます。さらに、**イルカ**には**ラビング**と呼ばれる**触覚によるコミュニケーション**もあります。**ラビング**とは胸ビレで相手の体を触り、片方もしくは両方の個体が動くことで体が擦(す)られる行動です。これにより、**個体同士の親密さを深めるという役割がある**ようです。

本文でも登場した、**鳥のさえずり**も動物の音声コミュニケーションの代表例です。**シジュウカラは発声のいろいろな要素を組み合わせて、複合的な意味を作っていること**を報告する論文があります。

問題 3

生物

普通種と希少種

別冊p.10／制限時間25分／470 words

解答

問1 **自然界には動植物の種類は豊富にあるが、そのうちの数種類で自然界のほとんどの個体数を占めていること。(49字)**

問2 **a seemingly contradictory conclusion**

問3 (3) **普通種は、希少種とちょうど同じくらい保護を必要としているかもしれない。**

(4) **工業型農業に、ヨーロッパで鳥がいなくなっていることの責任の大半がある。**

問4 (A) **い**　(B) **う**　(C) **お**　(D) **あ**

解説

問1

下線部(1) **自然はグラノーラのようだ**を具体的に説明せよという問題なので、どういう点でグラノーラのようなのかを説明する。コロンの後ろで具体化されているので、ここをまとめれば正解になる。

解法 POINT ❷ コロンの役割

コロンには、**前の抽象的な表現を後ろで具体化する働き**があります。前の抽象的な表現に下線部が引かれて、～字以内で説明しなさいという問題は頻出なので、しっかりとおさえておきましょう。

本問でも、like granolaを後ろで具体化している。**The list of ingredients is long, but the bowl is mostly filled with just a few of them.**「**材料のリストは長いが、それが入ったボウルは、そのうちごくわずかなものでしか満たされていないのがほとんどだ**」が具体化された表現。これを話題の自然に当てはめると、「**自然界には動植物の種類は豊富にあるが、そのうちの数種類で自然界のほとんどの個体数を占めていること**」が正解となる。

実際に、グラノーラは、オーツ麦、玄米、とうもろこしに加えて、メープルシロップ、オリーブオイル、ミックスナッツなどの材料がいくつも含まれているが、実質最初に挙げた穀物やミックスナッツなどがほとんどの比率を占めている。

問2

下線部(2) **a counter-intuitive idea「直観に反する考え」**は、下線部(3)の**common species may need protection just as much as rare ones do「普通種は希少種とちょうど同じくらい保護を必要としているかもしれない」**に対する表現。**第3段落第3文**に、**"The state of being common is rare."「普通である状態が珍しい」**と同じ趣旨の表現があり、それを手前で**a seemingly contradictory conclusion「一見すると矛盾している結論」**と説明しているので、これが正解。

問3

(3)

構文図解

common species (S) may need (V) protection (O) just as much (M) [as rare ones do] (M).

do：need protectionの代わりの代動詞
ones：speciesを受ける代名詞

common speciesがS、may needがV、protectionがOの第3文型の文。muchに**as～as...の比較表現**が使われており、**just「ちょうど」**という副詞が先頭のasを修飾しているので、「**…とちょうど同じくらい～**」となる。2つ目のas以下は、**onesがspeciesを受ける代名詞、doがneed protectionの代わりの代動詞**。以上を理解して日本語に訳すと、「**普通種は、希少種とちょうど同じくらい保護を必要としているかもしれない**」となる。

(4)

構文図解

Industrial agriculture (S) carries (V) much (O) (of the blame for Europe's disappearing birds) (M).

Industrial agricultureがS、carriesがV、muchがOの第3文型の文。ofから前置詞のカタマリが始まって、birdsまでの形容詞句を作り、muchを修飾する。以上を反映した「**工業型農業に、ヨーロッパで鳥がいなくなっていることの責任の大半がある**」が正解となる。

問4

（あ） すべてのものが珍しい

（い） 多くの普通種は、多くの希少種と同様にあまり研究されていない

（う） ヨーロッパで巣を作る鳥の数は、1980年以降、4億2100万羽減少した。その大陸全体の鳥の個体数のまる5分の1が消えたのだ

（え） その種は回復した

（お） この鳥類の減少は、まったくと言っていいほど普通種が原因で、その中には、ヒバリのような誰もが知る名前がある

空欄(A)を含む文は、～ , a paper published in ～ that found that **commonness was not a well-studied phenomenon**, and that (　A　).「**普通であることがしっかりと研究された現象ではなく、**(　A　)とわかった」という文。よって、「**普通であることがしっかりと研究された現象ではない**」と並列になるのは、**（い）many common species are as poorly studied as many rare ones**が正解とわかる。

続いて、空欄(B)、(C)を含む文は、Its authors found that (　B　), and that (　C　).となる。選択肢から、その著者が発見した目的語に当たる内容を探すと、(B)に**（う）the number of birds nesting in Europe has dropped by 421 million — fully one-fifth of the continent's bird population, gone — since 1980**と、(C)に**（お）this decline in sheer birdiness is accounted for almost entirely**

by common species, among them such household names as the skylarkが入るとわかる。特に(お)の**this decline**が、(う)の**the number of ～ has dropped**を受けている内容とわかれば、正解と特定できる。

最後に、空欄(D)を含む文は、前文から見ると、～ , **most of the common birds are declining toward scarcity. "The inevitable place you end up, " ～ "is that (　D　)."**「**その普通種のほとんどが、希少な状態に向かって数を減らしている。『最後に行きつく避けられない場所は、(　D　)**』～」である。**普通種の多くが希少な状態に向かうと、everything is rare. となる**ので、(あ)が正解。

構文図解

Nature is [like granola]: The list (of ingredients) is long, but the
S V 前置詞のlike M S ingredientsを指す M V C S
bowl is mostly filled with just a few (of them). Take England, [for
V O M V O M
example], [which is obsessed enough with animals and birds to count
M
its wildlife nearly one by one], population estimates (for 58 species of
形容詞 enough to do S 「個体数の概算」 M
land mammal in that country), [ranging from the familiar to the
分詞構文
obscure], total about 173 million animals. But just three species —
V O S
the common shrew, rabbit, and mole — account for half (of those
S′ イングランドの1億7300万の動物 V O M
individuals). [All told], the most common 25 percent (of English
M「全体的に見ると」 S M
mammal species) add up to 97 percent (of all the individual
V O M
animals). Similar patterns play out [on land] and [at sea], [in your
S V M M M
local park] or [across whole continents], and [whether you are
M 副詞節のwhether「AだろうとBだろうと」
counting beetles, shellfish, or tropical trees]. The most common land
M S
bird (in the United States and Canada) is the American robin,
M V C 同格のカンマ「すなわち」
harbinger (of spring). Robins alone are as numerous [as the two
M S V C M
countries' 277 least-common bird species combined].
コマツグミがアメリカやカナダで多数生息していること

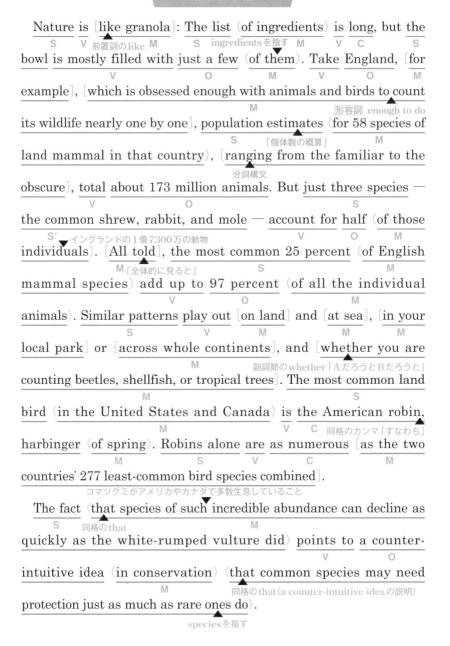

The fact 〈that species of such incredible abundance can decline as
S 同格のthat M
quickly as the white-rumped vulture did〉 points to a counter-
V O
intuitive idea (in conservation) 〈that common species may need
M 同格のthat(a counter-intuitive ideaの説明)
protection just as much as rare ones do〉.
speciesを指す

本文訳

自然はグラノーラのようだ。材料のリストは長いが、それが入ったボウルは、そのうちごくわずかなものでしか満たされていないのがほとんどだ。例えば、イングランドを取り上げてみると、そこは野生動物をほぼ1つ1つ数えるほど、動物や鳥に取りつかれているが、なじみのあるものから人目につかないものまで、その国の陸生の哺乳動物の58種の個体数の*概算は、合計で1億7,300万の動物がいることになる。しかし、よくあるトガリネズミ、ウサギ、そしてモグラのたった3種が、その個体数の半分を占めている。全体的に見ると、イギリスの哺乳動物の種の最もよくある25%が、合計してそのすべての動物の個体数の97%になる。陸地や海、近くの公園や大陸全体、そして*甲虫目(こうちゅうもく)、甲殻類、熱帯雨林の樹木を数えようと、似たようなパターンが見られる。アメリカやカナダの最もよくある陸生の鳥は、春を告げるコマツグミだ。コマツグミだけで、その2ヵ国の277の希少種の鳥を合計したのと同じくらいの数がいる。

そのような信じられないほど多数いる種が、ベンガルハゲワシと同じくらい急速に減少する可能性があるという事実は、自然保護という点において、普通種が希少種とちょうど同じくらい保護を必要としているかもしれないという直観に反する考えを暗示している。

*「概算」とは、おおよその計算のこと。

*「甲虫目」とは、カブトムシなど、甲冑(かっちゅう)のように厚く堅い前羽で体を保護している昆虫の種類。

語彙リスト

granola	名	グラノーラ(シリアルの一種)
ingredient	名	材料
be obsessed with	熟	～にとりつかれる
wildlife	名	野生生物
estimate	名	概算
obscure	形	人目につかない
total	動	合計～になる
mole	名	モグラ
account for	熟	～を占める
all told	熟	全体的に見て
add up to	熟	合計～になる
play out	熟	起こる
beetle	名	甲虫目
shellfish	名	甲殻類
incredible	形	信じられないほどの
abundance	名	大量
decline	動	減少する
rump	名	しり
vulture	名	ハゲワシ
point to	熟	暗示する
counter-intuitive	形	直感に反する
conservation	名	自然保護
protection	名	保護

▶単語10回CHECK 1 2 3 4 5 6 7 8 9 10

1 環境 2 生物 3 生物 4 環境 5 健康 6 文化 7 学問 8 生物 9 文化 10 社会

構文図解

The first scientist (to propose the conservation of the common)
S　不定詞 形容詞的用法　M

was, almost too perfectly, the author (of a book called *Rarity*). [After
V　M　C　M　分詞の後置修飾　M

20 years of studying what made some species rare], Kevin Gaston,
関係代名詞の what　S　同格のカンマ

an ecologist at the University of Exeter, in England, started ⟨to
M　V

wonder why other species are widespread and abundant⟩. He soon
不定詞 名詞的用法　O　S　M

came [to a seemingly contradictory conclusion] : "The state (of being
V　M　S　M

common) is rare." [While any given common species is made up of
V　C　M

many individuals], only a small fraction (of species) are common.
S　M　V　C

Gaston's work culminated [in "Common Ecology]," a paper
S　V　M　M′

published in the journal BioScience in 2011 that found that
過去分詞の名詞修飾　関係代名詞の that　名詞節の that

commonness was not a well-studied phenomenon, and that "many
found の目的語の that 節を接続　名詞節の that

common species are as poorly studied as many rare ones." The work
species を指す　S

triggered a quiet increase (in research). A study (from 2014) hints at
V　O　M　S　M　V

the scale (of what has been overlooked). Its authors found ⟨that the
O　関係代名詞　M　S　V　名詞節の that　O

number of birds nesting in Europe has dropped by 421 million —
分詞の後置修飾

fully one-fifth of the continent's bird population, gone — since 1980,
one-fifth が主語の分詞構文

and that this decline in sheer birdiness is accounted for almost
found の目的語の that 節を接続

entirely by common species, among them such household names as
common species を指す　such A as B

the skylark⟩.

本文訳

普通種の保存を提案した最初の科学者が、レアリティと呼ばれる本の作者だというのはほぼ完璧すぎるほどの事象だ。ある種が希少になった原因を20年間研究した後に、イギリスのエクスター大学の生態学者であるケビン・ガストンは、なぜ他の種が広がって数多くなっているのかと疑問に思い始めた。彼は一見すると矛盾している「普通である状態が珍しい」という結論にすぐに達した。いかなる特定の普通種も多くの個体から構成されているが、種の中でほんのわずかな一部しか普通ではない。

ガストンの研究は、ついには「コモン・エコロジー」という論文となった。その論文は2011年のバイオサイエンス誌に掲載されたが、それによって普通であることがしっかりと研究された現象ではなく、「多くの普通種は、多くの希少種と同様にあまり研究されていない」とわかった。その研究は、静かながら研究を増加させるきっかけとなった。2014年からの研究は、見過ごされてきたものの大きさを示唆するものだ。その著者たちは、ヨーロッパで巣を作る鳥の数が、1980年以降、4億2100万羽減少したこと、それはその大陸の鳥の個体数のまる5分の1が消えたことであり、そしてこの鳥類の減少は、まったくと言っていいほど普通種（の減少）が原因で、その中には、ヒバリのような誰もが知る名前もあることがわかった。

語彙リスト

ecologist	名 生態学者
seemingly	副 一見すると
contradictory	形 矛盾した
conclusion	名 結論
given	形 特定の
be made up of	熟 ～で構成されている
fraction	名 少し
culminate in	熟 ついには～となる
paper	名 論文
phenomenon	名 現象
commonness	名 普通であること
trigger	動 ～のきっかけとなる
hint at	熟 ほのめかす
overlook	動 見過ごす
nest	動 巣を作る
sheer	形 純粋な
birdiness	名 鳥類
household name	名 誰もが知る名前
skylark	名 ヒバリ

▸単語10回CHECK 1 2 3 4 5 6 7 8 9 10

構文図解

Industrial agriculture carries much (of the blame for Europe's disappearing birds). "They've been taking out hedgerows, taking out trees, making fields bigger, increasing inputs of pesticides — just essentially squeezing out the opportunities for wild organisms to live in those kinds of environments," Gaston told me. "We're talking just massive losses."

S: Industrial agriculture / V: carries / O: much / M: (of the blame for Europe's disappearing birds)

They: industrial agricultureの人々を指す

O_2: hedgerows ～ environments

for wild organisms: 不定詞の主語

to live: 不定詞 形容詞的用法 the opportunitiesを修飾

S: Gaston / V: told / O_1: me. S: We / V: 're talking / O: just massive losses

But even the most human-adapted and urban (of birds), (such as starlings and house sparrows), have steeply decreased — [in fact], those two very common birds were [among the top five birds experiencing population declines]. Most (of the rarest birds in Europe) are actually increasing [at present], [due to successful conservation efforts], [although they remain uncommon]; meanwhile, most (of the common birds) are declining [toward scarcity]. "The inevitable place you end up," said Gaston, "is that everything is rare."

S: even the most human-adapted and urban / M: (of birds) / M: (such as starlings and house sparrows) / V: have steeply decreased / M: [in fact]

those: starlings, house sparrowsを指す

S: those two very common birds / V: were / M: [among the top five birds experiencing population declines]

experiencing: 分詞の後置修飾

S: Most / M: (of the rarest birds in Europe) / V: are actually increasing / M: [at present] / M: [due to successful conservation efforts] / M: [although they remain uncommon] / M: meanwhile

they: the rarest birds in Europeを指す

S: most / M: (of the common birds) / V: are declining / M: [toward scarcity]

O: The inevitable place you end up / V: said / S: Gaston

place you: 関係詞の省略

that: 名詞節のthat

本文訳

*工業型農業に、ヨーロッパで鳥がいなくなっていることの責任の大半がある。「彼らは、生垣や木々を取り除き、平野をより大きくして、農薬の散布を増やして、野生生物がそうした類の環境で生息する機会を根本からなくしてきた」とガストンは私に教えてくれた。「私たちはまさに大量の損失について話をしている」と。

しかし、ムクドリやスズメのような最も人間に慣れていて都会的な鳥でさえ、急激に減少している。実際に、それら2つのよくある鳥は、個体数の減少を経験している上位5種の鳥のうちの一部だ。ヨーロッパの最も希少な鳥のほとんどは、まだ普通ではないが、保護努力がうまくいったおかげで、現在は実際には増えている。一方で、普通種のほとんどが、希少(きしょう)な状態に向かって数を減らしている。「最後に行きつく避けられない場所は、すべてが希少になることだ」とガストンは言った。

*「工業型農業」とは、農産物などを産業的に生産する近代的な農業体系のことを指す。高い生産性がある一方で、様々な環境問題を作り出してきたので、現在では環境に配慮した持続可能な農業を目指す「循環型農業」という概念が生まれている。

語彙リスト

take out	熟 取り除く	sparrow	名 スズメ
hedgerow	名 生け垣	steeply	副 急激に
pesticide	名 農薬	among	前 ~の1つ
squeeze out	熟 締め出す	meanwhile	副 一方で
organism	名 生き物	scarcity	名 欠乏
massive	形 大量の	inevitable	形 避けられない
starling	名 ムクドリ	end up	熟 最後には~になる

▶単語10回CHECK 1 2 3 4 5 6 7 8 9 10

Nature is like granola: The list of ingredients is long, but the bowl is mostly filled with just a few of them. Take England, for example, which is obsessed enough with animals and birds to count its wildlife nearly one by one, population estimates for 58 species of land mammal in that country, ranging from the familiar to the obscure, total about 173 million animals. But just three species — the common shrew, rabbit, and mole — account for half of those individuals. All told, the most common 25 percent of English mammal species add up to 97 percent of all the individual animals. Similar patterns play out on land and at sea, in your local park or across whole continents, and whether you are counting beetles, shellfish, or tropical trees. The most common land bird in the United States and Canada is the American robin, harbinger of spring. Robins alone are as numerous as the two countries' 277 least-common bird species combined.

The fact that species of such incredible abundance can decline as quickly as the white-rumped vulture did points to a counter-intuitive idea in conservation that common species may need protection just as much as rare ones do.

The first scientist to propose the conservation of the common was, almost too perfectly, the author of a book called *Rarity*. After 20 years of studying what made some species rare, Kevin Gaston, an ecologist at the University of Exeter, in England, started to wonder why other species are widespread and abundant. He soon came to a seemingly contradictory conclusion: "The state of being common is rare." While any given common species is made up of many individuals, only a small fraction of species are common.

Gaston's work culminated in "Common Ecology," a paper published in the journal BioScience in 2011 that found that commonness was not a well-studied phenomenon, and that "many common species are as poorly studied as many rare ones." The work triggered a quiet increase in research. A study from 2014 hints at the scale of what has been overlooked. Its authors found that the number of birds nesting in Europe has dropped by 421 million — fully one-fifth of the continent's bird population, gone — since 1980, and that this decline in sheer birdiness is accounted for almost entirely by common species, among them such household names as the skylark.

Industrial agriculture carries much of the blame for Europe's disappearing birds. "They've been taking out hedgerows, taking out trees, making fields bigger, increasing inputs of pesticides — just essentially squeezing out the opportunities for wild organisms to live in those kinds of environments," Gaston told me. "We're talking just massive losses."

But even the most human-adapted and urban of birds, such as starlings and house sparrows, have steeply decreased — in fact, those two very common birds were among the top five birds experiencing population declines. Most of the rarest birds in Europe are actually increasing at present, due to successful conservation efforts, although they remain uncommon; meanwhile, most of the common birds are declining toward scarcity. "The inevitable place you end up," said Gaston, "is that everything is rare."

▸音読10回CHECK 1 2 3 4 5 6 7 8 9 10

背景知識が広がるコラム

BACKGROUND KNOWLEDGE

絶滅危惧種

そもそも、**希少種や絶滅危惧種をなぜ保護しなければいけないのか**、それを考えるとき、**生物多様性**というキーワードが浮かんできます。多種多様な野生生物がつながり合って形づくられている**生物多様性**によって、豊かな自然が維持されています。**生物多様性に富んだ自然**は水や食料、木材、繊維、医薬品など、私たち人間が**生きていくのに不可欠な資源を提供**してくれます。しかし近年、**開発による環境破壊、乱獲**のような人間の行為により野生生物が絶滅し、**生物多様性が失われつつあります**。それを防ぐために様々な取り組みが行われています。

その一環として、1973年に採択された**ワシントン条約**があります。背景には、1960年代以降、アフリカで横行した、角や牙を狙ったサイやゾウなどの大規模な密猟があります。ゾウの牙である**象牙**や、**サイの角**、**生きたオウムやトカゲ**、**カメ**などが、高値で取り引きされました。これを防ぐために、国際取引を規制することで、**無秩序な乱獲などから絶滅危惧種を保護**するために、国際取引を規制したのがワシントン条約です。

日本国内では、**トキ**、**コウノトリ**、**イリオモテヤマネコ**などの保全の取り組みを耳にしたことがある人も多いでしょう。トキは里山を生息地とした鳥ですが、乱獲や生息環境の悪化によって、**野生のトキは絶滅**してしまいました。2008年に、佐渡島で**人工繁殖**した10羽のトキを自然に放つことに成功してから、野生復帰の取り組みが進められています。

コウノトリも1971年に絶滅しましたが、1989年に人工繁殖に成功して、それ以降野生復帰の取り組みが推進されています。沖縄・**西表島**(いりおもてじま)だけに生息する野生のネコである**イリオモテヤマネコ**も、**国の特別天然記念物**であり、**絶滅危惧種の1つ**です。イリオモテヤマネコを守ることで生物多様性を維持し、西表島の自然を守ることにつなげようと、様々な取り組みが行われています。

問題 4

環境

プラスチックごみ問題

別冊p.14 ／制限時間25分／549 words

解答

(1) b	(2) a	(3) c	(4) b	(5) b
(6) a	(7) b	(8) c	(9) d	(10) c

解説

(1)

この文章の (1) 優先順位という単語は（　　　）を意味している可能性が最も高い。

(a)　人間のアルコール消費量をコントロールする方法
(b)　物事をその重要度で配列する方式
(c)　人間の様々な成功レベルを決める公式
(d)　必要性よりも人間の貪欲(どんよく)さから生まれる無秩序な状態

hierarchy「**階層制度**」が、本問では「**優先順位**」の意味で使われているので、**(b) a system in which things are arranged by their importance** が正解。

(2)

第2段落の文脈に基づいて、(2)（　　　）に最もよく合う単語を選びなさい。

(a)　競合する　　(b)　感じのよい
(c)　邪魔をする　　(d)　目的のある

空欄(2)を含む文をまとめると、「したがって、24時間常にいくつもの (2)（　　　）問題が生じる政治の世界で、私たちの健康に関係する懸念事項が、社会の優先リストの最上位にくるのは驚くことではない」となる。すると、「**重要度を競い合う問題がいくつもある中で**」という文脈なので、**(a) competing** が正解。

(3)

第3段落で、筆者は重要な問題の解決が可能になるのは、それらの問題が（　　　）ときだと示唆する。

(a)　直接的な方法で、影響力のある政治家の生活を変える
(b)　地元の医師の助言を通じて、大衆の認識を変える
(c)　不都合な方法で人類に影響を与えるものと提示される
(d)　『Slow Death by Rubber Duck』のような本で議論される

第3段落で、**once an issue transforms into a human health concern**, it becomes far more likely to be taken up by our elected leaders, ~ and consequently solved.「**一度ある問題が人間の健康上の懸念に変わると**、私たちが選んだリーダーに取り上げられ、~その結果**解決される**可能性がはるかに高くなる」から、(c) **are presented as affecting humanity in an unfavorable way** が正解。本文の**transforms into a human health concern**が、(c)の**are presented as affecting humanity in an unfavorable way**と同義であることに注意する。

---

(4)

第4段落の文脈に基づいて、下線部(4)の文の意味で可能性が高いのは、タバコ会社が（　　　）ことだ。

(a)　その活動に反対するのに成功した
(b)　最終的に変化に屈しなければならなかった
(c)　現状を効果的に維持した
(d)　この改革を積極的に支持した

下線部(4)を構文図解で解説する。

構文図解

the momentum (S) (for change) (M) became (V) impossible (C) [for even the most defiant cigarette companies to resist] (M).

for even the most defiant cigarette companies: 不定詞の主語
to resist: 不定詞 副詞的用法 形容詞修飾（impossibleを修飾）

the momentumがS、becameがV、impossibleがCの第2文型の文。**for ~ companiesは不定詞to resistの主語。to resistは不定詞の副詞的用法・形容詞修飾なので、「抵抗するのは不可能になった」と**

impossibleを修飾する。まとめると、「**変革への勢いによって、最も反抗的なタバコ会社ですら抵抗するのが不可能になった**」となるので、(b) **eventually had to give in to change**が正解。**became impossible ~ to resist**が、**had to give in to change**にパラフレーズされていることに注意する。

構文 POINT ❷ 不定詞の副詞的用法・形容詞修飾

不定詞の副詞的用法・形容詞修飾は、不定詞の多岐にわたる用法でも、最も難易度が高いものです。例文をご覧ください。

（例文）

This river is dangerous **to swim in.**

訳 この川は、泳ぐには危険だ。

to swim inが**不定詞の副詞的用法・形容詞修飾**で、「**泳ぐには**」の意味でdangerousを修飾します。この用法を特定するには、① **難易形容詞（hard, difficult, dangerous, impossible, easyなど）**が使われ、② **不定詞の目的語が欠けている**という特徴があります。例文でもdangerousが使われて、swim inの目的語が欠けています。

本問でも、impossible「**不可能だ**」は**極めて難しい**ことなので、**難易形容詞**と判断する。resistの目的語が欠けているので、**不定詞の副詞的用法・形容詞修飾**と判断して正解を導く。

(5)

第5段落では (5) 浸透するという単語は、（　　　）を意味している可能性が最も高い。

(a)　罰する　　(b)　中に入る

(c)　支配する　(d)　イライラさせる

permeatingは「**浸透する**」の意味で、本問では「人間の体に**侵入する**」という文脈で使われているので、一番近い **(b) entering**が正解。

語彙 POINT ❹ perはthrough「～を通って」の意味

persist ／ perfume ／ permeate

perにはthrough「～を通って」の意味があります。**per「～を通って」＋ sist「立つ」＝「ずっと動かずに立っている」＝ persist「固執する」**となります。**per「～を通って」＋ fume「煙」＝「良い香りの煙を通して神に祈る」**行為から、**perfume「香水」**となりました。**per「～を通って」＋ meate「行く」＝ permeate「浸透する」**になります。

(6)

第6段落で、次のうち**当てはまらない**のはどれか。

(a) これらの粒子は、ごく限られた数の製品で発見された。
(b) 水に長くさらされているにも関わらず、プラスチックは鉱化したり、消えてなくなったりすることはない。
(c) 水道水のほとんどが、これらの粒子で汚染されている国もある。
(d) プラスチックの粒子はとても微小なので、裸眼では目に見えない。

第6段落第4文 In ～, scientists have started to **find these particles in an astonishing range of products** including … .「～で、科学者は、…を含んだ**驚くほど多くの種類の製品に、これらの粒子を発見**し始めた」**と (a) は反する**ので、正解。

不正解の選択肢を見ていくと、(b)は、**同段落第1文 Plastic, it turns out, never really disappears.** から推論できるので不適。(c)は、**同段落最終文 In ～, 83 per cent of tap water in seven countries was found to contain plastic micro-fibres.** と一致するので不適。(d)は、**同段落第2文 In ～, it just gets mushed into smaller and smaller bits.**、**同段落第3文 These microscopic particles ～.** から推論できるので不適。

(7)

第7・第8段落の内容に基づいて、(7)(　　　)に最も適切な答えを選びなさい。

(a) 決してない　(b) ちょっと
(c) 本当ではない　(d) むしろ

空欄(7)の前後の文をまとめると、「ウミガメが、毎日使う買い物袋で窒息死していることを、私が気にするか？ (7)(　　　)。しかし、自分の身に不都合が生じるほどではないのは確かだ」から、**少しは気にかけるが、自分の身に不都合が生じるほどではない**と文脈を読み取れるので、**(b) Sort of**が正解。

(8)

第7～9段落で、筆者は、面倒なことが原因で、人は(　　　)場合を除いて、プラスチック問題に対して行動をとることを避ける傾向にあると示唆しているように思える。

(a) 雪が解けて、プラスチックごみがあらわになる
(b) オーガニックフードは食べるのに安全ではないと、研究が裏づける
(c) 最愛の人が深刻な影響を受けると、証拠で示される
(d) 海洋のプラスチックが膨大すぎて無視できなくなる

第9段落第1文で、筆者の2人の息子が、**体に埋め込まれたプラスチック粒子が原因で前立腺がんを患う可能性が劇的に高まるなら関心を示す**とあるので、**(c) evidence shows that it will seriously impact loved ones**が正解。同文の**my two boysが (c)のloved ones と同義**で、同文の**have a dramatically increased chance of contracting prostate cancer**が(c)の**will seriously impact**にパラフレーズされていることに注意する。

(9)

第10段落において、筆者によると、この大きな問題への解決策は何か。

(a) 私たちは、より優れた再利用のテクノロジーを開発するのにもっと資金を投資すべきだ。
(b) 私たちは、衣料品メーカーが合成繊維を使うことを禁止しなければならない。
(c) 私たちは、プラスチック製品を適切に処理するのに、収納ユニッ

トを作るべきだ。
(d) 私たちは、プラスチックの製造と使用を最終的に終わらせなければならない。

第10段落第3文 The issue is **our society's addiction to plastic itself**.「問題は、**私たちの社会のプラスチックへの依存そのもの**だ」や、**第10段落最終文** It's not just the plastic we're throwing away that's the problem; **it's the plastic items we surround ourselves with every day**.「問題は、私たちが捨てているプラスチックだけではなく、**日々私たちの周りに存在するプラスチック製品なのだ**」から、**プラスチック製品の使用を控えて減らさなければいけない**とわかる。**(d) We must ultimately put an end to the production and use of plastic.** が最も近いので正解となる。

(10)

筆者は、この文章の中の (10) 有毒な氷山の一角にすぎないというフレーズで、何を意味しているか。
(a) その高さのせいで、この問題の解決策に手が届かないこと。
(b) 微粒子に関するこの新しい科学は、かなり印象的であること。
(c) この情報は、破滅的な全体のわずかな部分だということ。
(d) 氷山の一角が、この問題を抑制する手がかりを与えてくれること。

下線部(10)を含む文は、The new science on plastic micro-particles is stunning and I'm guessing (10) only the tip of a toxic iceberg.「プラスチックの微粒子に関する新しい科学は、驚くべきもので、**有毒な氷山の一角に過ぎない**と私は考えている」となる。**マイクロプラスチックは、大きな問題のほんの一部に過ぎない**ことを表現しているとわかるので、**(c) That this information is a minute part of a destructive whole.** が正解となる。

不正解の選択肢を見ていくと、(a)は、**その問題の大きさのせいで解決できないと言っているのではない**ので、不適。(b)は **rather impressive「かなり印象的」という問題ではない**ので不適。(d)は**氷山の一角が問題への手がかりを与えてくれる話ではない**ので不適。

構文図解

[In the hierarchy of human needs], good health is [right at the
M S V M
top]. There's a reason (we say, "to your health," whenever we clink
M V S 関係詞の省略 M
glasses).

付帯状況の with
[In the complicated world of politics], therefore, [with numerous
M M M
competing issues coming at us 24 hours a day], it's not surprising
分詞の名詞修飾 with O C の C S V C
〈that concerns clearly relevant to our health and that of our families
名詞節の that S′ 形容詞の後置修飾 health を指す
regularly rise to the top of our society's priority list〉. The effect (of
concerns に対する V S
plastic on our health) should be [at the top of that list] today.
M V M M

[As Bruce Lourie and I explain in our book Slow Death by Rubber
様態の as M 人間の健康上の懸念に変わった問題
Duck], [once an issue transforms into a human health concern], it
「一度 S が V すると」 M S
becomes far more likely to be taken up [by our elected leaders],
V M
noticed [by the general public] and consequently solved.
V M taken, noticed, solved の3つの接続 M V

The smoking debate followed this path. [Once the focus became the
S V O 「一度 S が V すると」 M
damaging effects of second-hand smoke, i.e., it's not just the health of
「すなわち」 S V C
smokers at risk but the health of all those around them], the
not just A but(also) B 「人々」の意味 smokers を指す S
momentum (for change) became impossible [for even the most
M V C 不定詞の主語 M
defiant cigarette companies to resist].
不定詞 副詞的用法 形容詞修飾 (impossible を修飾)

本文訳

人間が必要とすることの優先順位では、健康でいることがまさに一番にくる。私たちが乾杯するとき、「あなたの健康を祝して」と言うには理由がある。

したがって、政治の複雑な世界で、無数の競合する問題が1日24時間私たちの身に押し寄せる中で、自分たちや家族の健康に明らかに関係する重要な事柄が、定期的に社会の優先項目のリストの一番上に浮上するのは驚きではない。私たちの健康に及ぼすプラスチックの影響は、現代のそのリストの一番上に位置しているはずだ。

ブルース・ローリーと私が共著の『Slow Death by Rubber Duck』で説明したように、一度ある問題が人間の健康上の懸念に変わると、私たちが選んだリーダーに取り上げられ、一般大衆にも注目され、その結果解決される可能性がはるかに高くなる。

喫煙の論争がこの道筋をたどった。一度その焦点が副流煙の有害な影響にあてられると、すなわちそれは単に喫煙者の健康だけでなく、その周りの人みんなの健康も危険な状態にあるということなので、変革への勢いによって、最も反抗的なタバコ会社ですら抵抗するのが不可能になった。

語彙リスト

hierarchy	名 優先順位
clink glasses	熟 乾杯する
complicated	形 複雑な
competing	形 競合する
come at	熟 押し寄せる
relevant to	熟 ～に関係する
priority	名 優先事項
once S V	接 一度SがVすると
transform into	熟 ～に変わる
take up	熟 取り上げる
general public	名 一般大衆
consequently	副 結果として
second-hand smoke	名 副流煙
momentum	名 勢い
defiant	形 反抗的な

▸単語10回CHECK 1 2 3 4 5 6 7 8 9 10

構文図解

〈What we are witnessing now〉 is the genesis (of another human health problem that I believe has the potential to dominate public debate over the next decade) : the discovery that tiny plastic particles are permeating every human on earth.

関係代名詞の what　S　V　C　M
連鎖関係詞「～な可能性があると私が思う問題」　不定詞 形容詞的用法
同格の that

元々は It turns out that plastic never really disappears. の文

Plastic, it turns out, never really disappears. [In response to time and sunlight, or the action of waves], it just gets mushed [into smaller and smaller bits]. These microscopic particles then enter the food chain, air and soil. [In the past couple of years], scientists have started 〈to find these particles in an astonishing range of products including table salt and honey, bottled and tap water, shellfish and ... beer〉. [In one recent study], 83 per cent (of tap water in seven countries) was found [to contain plastic micro-fibres].

M　S　V　M
plastic を指す　S　M　V　C　M
プラスチックが粉々になったもの　S　M　V　O
M　S　V
不定詞 名詞的用法　O
「～を含んで」
M　S　M
V　to do

[When the snow melts in Canada to reveal a winter's worth of Tim Hortons' cups and lids], every person (in this country) notices the plastic litter (that surrounds us). Many (of us) know [of the vast and accumulating patches of garbage in the ocean]. I hear shoppers (in the produce aisles of my local grocery store) grumbling [at the increasing size of the plastic that encases the organic arugula].

M　不定詞 副詞的用法 結果
S　M　V　O
関係代名詞の that　M　S　M　V　M
S　V　O
M　C
M　関係代名詞の that

本文訳

今、私たちが目にしているのは、私が次の十年で大衆の議論を支配する可能性があると思う、もう1つの人間の健康問題の起源となるものだ。それは、微小なプラスチックの粒子が、地球上のあらゆる人間の体に侵入しているという発見だ。

プラスチックは、実際には決して消えることがないとわかっている。時間や太陽光、波の作用に反応して、プラスチックは、どんどん細かく砕かれるだけだ。これらの顕微鏡でしか見えない粒子は、次に食物連鎖、空気、土壌に入っていく。過去数年で、科学者は、食卓塩、はちみつ、ペットボトルの水、水道水、貝類、そしてビールなどを含んだ驚くほど多くの種類の製品の中に、これらの粒子を発見し始めた。ある最近の研究では、7ヵ国の水道水の83%が、プラスチックのマイクロファイバーを含んでいることがわかった。

カナダで雪が溶けて、ひと冬分の*ティム・ホートンズのカップや蓋(ふた)があらわになると、この国のすべての人が、自分たちを取り囲むプラスチックごみに気付く。私たちの多くが、海にある膨大な蓄積しているごみの山について知っている。近くの食料品店の農作物の売り場の買い物客が、無農薬の*ルッコラを入れるプラスチックのサイズが大きくなっていることに文句を言っているのを、私は耳にする。

*ティム・ホートンズ（Tim Hortons）は、カナダの有名なドーナツチェーン店。

*「ルッコラ」は、葉をサラダなどに使うアブラナ科の植物。

語彙リスト

witness	動	目撃する
genesis	名	起源
potential	名	可能性
dominate	動	支配する
tiny	形	微小な
particle	名	粒子
permeate	動	浸透（侵入）する
mush	動	粉々に砕く
bit	名	かけら
food chain	名	食物連鎖
astonishing	形	驚くほどの
tap water	名	水道水
shellfish	名	貝類、甲殻類
micro-fiber	名	マイクロファイバー（繊維のこと）
lid	名	ふた
litter	名	ごみ
accumulate	動	蓄積する
patch	名	区画
produce	名	農作物
aisle	名	通路
grumble at	熟	～について不平を言う
encase	動	～を入れる
arugula	名	ルッコラ

▸単語10回CHECK 1 2 3 4 5 6 7 8 9 10

構文図解

None (of this), really, matters much. Do I care 〈that sea turtles are choking to death on the plastic grocery bags I use every day〉? Sort of. But certainly not enough to inconvenience myself.

S M M V M S V 名詞節のthat O 関係詞の省略 M M

海洋のプラスチックごみの存在や買い物客のプラスチックの包みへの文句を耳にすることなど

But [if it turns out that my two boys have a dramatically increased chance of contracting prostate cancer because of all the plastic particles that are implanted in their growing bodies], now you've got my attention. Make it stop, please.

it turns out that ~「~とわかる」 M 関係代名詞のthat プラスチック問題 M S V O V O C M

Forget recycling. We can't recycle ourselves [out of this problem]. The issue is our society's addiction (to plastic itself). Those plastic micro-fibres (I mentioned)? Scientists are now saying 〈that one of the primary sources in our drinking water is the lint that comes off the synthetic fabric of our clothing〉. It's not just the plastic we're throwing away that's the problem; it's the plastic items we surround ourselves with every day.

V O S V O M プラスチック問題 S V C M 関係詞の省略 M S V 名詞節のthat O 関係代名詞のthat 関係詞の省略 強調構文 関係詞の省略

The new science (on plastic micro-particles) is stunning and I'm guessing only the tip (of a toxic iceberg).

S M V C S V O M

本文訳

このどれもが、実際には大して重要ではない。私が毎日使うプラスチックの買い物袋でウミガメが窒息死しているのを、私は気にかけるだろうか？　多少は気にかける。しかし、自分の身に不都合が起きるほど気にかけないのは確かだ。

しかし、もし私の2人の息子が、成長期の体に埋め込まれたあらゆるプラスチック粒子が原因で前立腺がんを患う可能性が劇的に高まるとわかるなら、私の注意を引き付けただろう。お願いだから、それを止めよう。

再利用を忘れなさい。私たちは、自分自身を再生してこの問題から抜け出すことはできない。問題は、私たちの社会のプラスチックへの依存そのものだ。私が言ったそうしたプラスチックのマイクロファイバーは？　科学者は現在、飲み水のマイクロファイバーの主要な原因の1つが、私たちの衣服の合成繊維から剥(は)がれ落ちる糸くずだと言っている。問題は、私たちが捨てているプラスチックだけではなく、日々私たちの周りに存在するプラスチック製品なのだ。

プラスチックの微粒子に関する新しい科学は、驚くべきもので、有毒な氷山の一角に過ぎないと私は考えている。

語彙リスト

matter	動 重要である	primary	形 主要な
sea turtle	名 ウミガメ	lint	名 糸くず
choke to death	熟 窒息死する	come off	熟 ～から離れる
grocery bag	名 買い物袋	synthetic	形 合成の
inconvenience	動 不便をかける	fabric	名 繊維
it turns out that ~	熟 ～とわかる	throw away	熟 捨てる
contract	動 （病気に）かかる	stunning	形 驚くべき
prostate cancer	名 前立腺がん	tip	名 先端
implant	動 埋め込む	toxic	形 有毒な
addiction to	熟 ～依存、～中毒	iceberg	名 氷山

▸単語10回CHECK 1 2 3 4 5 6 7 8 9 10

In the hierarchy of human needs, good health is right at the top. There's a reason we say, "to your health," whenever we clink glasses.

In the complicated world of politics, therefore, with numerous competing issues coming at us 24 hours a day, it's not surprising that concerns clearly relevant to our health and that of our families regularly rise to the top of our society's priority list. The effect of plastic on our health should be at the top of that list today.

As Bruce Lourie and I explain in our book Slow Death by Rubber Duck, once an issue transforms into a human health concern, it becomes far more likely to be taken up by our elected leaders, noticed by the general public and consequently solved.

The smoking debate followed this path. Once the focus became the damaging effects of second-hand smoke, i.e., it's not just the health of smokers at risk but the health of all those around them, the momentum for change became impossible for even the most defiant cigarette companies to resist.

What we are witnessing now is the genesis of another human health problem that I believe has the potential to dominate public debate over the next decade: the discovery that tiny plastic particles are permeating every human on earth.

Plastic, it turns out, never really disappears. In response to time and sunlight, or the action of waves, it just gets mushed into smaller and smaller bits. These microscopic particles then enter the food chain, air and soil. In the past couple of years, scientists have started to find these particles in an astonishing range of products including table salt and honey, bottled and tap water, shellfish and ... beer. In one recent study, 83 per cent of tap water in seven countries was found to contain plastic micro-fibres.

When the snow melts in Canada to reveal a winter's worth of Tim Hortons' cups and lids, every person in this country notices the plastic litter that surrounds us. Many of us know of the vast and accumulating patches of garbage in the ocean. I hear shoppers in the produce aisles of my local grocery store grumbling at the increasing size of the plastic that encases the organic arugula.

None of this, really, matters much. Do I care that sea turtles are choking to death on the plastic grocery bags I use every day? Sort of. But certainly not enough to inconvenience myself.

But if it turns out that my two boys have a dramatically increased chance of contracting prostate cancer because of all the plastic particles that are implanted in their growing bodies, now you've got my attention. Make it stop, please.

Forget recycling. We can't recycle ourselves out of this problem. The issue is our society's addiction to plastic itself. Those plastic micro-fibres I mentioned? Scientists are now saying that one of the primary sources in our drinking water is the lint that comes off the synthetic fabric of our clothing. It's not just the plastic we're throwing away that's the problem; it's the plastic items we surround ourselves with every day.

The new science on plastic micro-particles is stunning and I'm guessing only the tip of a toxic iceberg.

▸音読10回CHECK 1 2 3 4 5 6 7 8 9 10

背景知識が広がるコラム

BACKGROUND KNOWLEDGE

環境問題と公共心

前著の**『英語長文問題ソリューション』**でも、今作の**『英語長文問題ソリューション最新テーマ編』**でも、**プラスチックごみによる海洋汚染問題**を扱いました。プラスチックに関する問題は、近年の大きな関心事の1つです。プラスチックごみ問題に加えて、地球温暖化など、私たちはそもそも、**なぜ環境問題を考えなければいけないのでしょうか。**

まずは、本当に**現在の地球の環境は危機的状況にあること**、何らかの対策をしないと、**sustainable（持続可能）な社会ではなくなる**こと、何より、**私たちだけでなく次の世代が、大きなマイナスを被ってしまうこと**、すべてが環境問題を考える理由の答えになります。

私自身が環境問題を考える理由の1つに、**公共心**という考えがあります。**公共心**とは、**自分が社会の一員であることを認識して、自分のとる行動が社会に与えている影響を想像すること**を言います。この**公共心を意識することで、大きく個人の精神性は変わってきます。**私自身も、若いころは、環境問題のことなど考えたことはなく、今思い返すと恥ずかしくなるような利己的な行いばかりしていました。

現在では、幸いにも、大学入試の題材を読むなど、非常に多くの環境問題に触れる機会があります。**年齢を重ねるほどに、自分以外の世界を想像して、自分の行動を少しずつ律することができるようになってきました。**

まず身近でできることは、**ごみの分別をしっかり行うこと**です。**不燃ごみ、資源ごみと分けて、ペットボトルは洗ってキャップや周りのビニールを取ってリサイクルに出す**ようになりました。**地球温暖化に対して個人でできること**として、**車を手放して、公共交通機関を利用する**ようになりました。**公共心を意識することで得られる精神性や世界は、自分や周りのものを一段上のところへ導いてくれる**ものです。

問題 5

健康

椅子に座ることの弊害

別冊p.20／制限時間25分／541 words

解答

設問 1. b

設問 2. b

設問 3. （イ）a　（ロ）d　（ハ）a　（ニ）c

設問 4. **The risk remained, even if sitting was broken up by standing and walking.**

解説

設問 1.

(a) 1週間に最低5回運動する中年の成人は、早期死亡の割合が低くなることが報告されている。

(b) 研究によって、1日に9時間半じっと座っていることは、早期死亡のリスクを高めることがわかった。

(c) 最近の研究結果によると、適度な運動は、軽い、あるいは精力的な活動よりも健康によいということだ。

(d) 最近の科学報告書によると、若者は十分な運動をしておらず、1日ほぼ10時間座っているとされている。

空欄【あ】の次の文は、Middle-aged and older people who **live sedentary lives are** up to two and a half times **more likely to die early**, ～.「**座ってばかりの生活を送っている**中年の人、そしてそれより高齢の人は、2.5倍にまで**早期死亡する可能性が高くなる**～」である。この文が具体例に当たる(b) **Sitting still** for nine and a half hours a day **raises the risk of early death**, a study has found. が正解となる。**Sitting still** が **live sedentary lives**、**raises the risk of early death** が **are ～ more likely to die early に具体化されている**ことに気付くと、正解がすぐにわかる。

設問 2.

(a) (ⅰ) 2,149 (ⅱ) 62 (ⅲ) 40 (ⅳ) 36,400
(b) (ⅰ) 36,400 (ⅱ) 40 (ⅲ) 62 (ⅳ) 2,149
(c) (ⅰ) 36,400 (ⅱ) 62 (ⅲ) 40 (ⅳ) 2,149
(d) (ⅰ) 2,149 (ⅱ) 40 (ⅲ) 62 (ⅳ) 36,400

空欄(ⅰ)と(ⅳ)の関係性に着目すると、**約(ⅰ)人の成人の身体活動や死亡率に関する研究を分析して、6年の追跡調査の間に、(ⅳ)人が亡くなったという関係性**である。したがって、**(ⅰ)のほうが、数字が大きい必要がある**ので、(b)と(c)に正解の候補を絞ることができる。

続いて、(ⅱ)と(ⅲ)の関係性に着目すると、**研究対象が(ⅱ)歳かそれ以上**で、**被験者の平均年齢が(ⅲ)歳**ということは、**(ⅱ)が(ⅲ)より数字が低い必要がある**ので、**(b)**が正解となる。

設問 3.

(イ)
(a) 急落した (b) ほどほどに増加した
(c) 不変なままだった (d) 劇的に増加した

空欄(イ)の前の文で、「**どんなレベルの身体活動でも、早期死亡のリスクをかなり下げることに関係している**」から、「**全体の活動が増えると死亡数は減る**」とわかるので、**(a) fell steeply**が正解。

(ロ)
(a) ～によると (b) ～に基づいて
(c) ～が原因で (d) ～に関係なく

第6段落第1文の～ **any level of physical activity was associated with a substantially lower risk of early death.**「**どんなレベルの身体活動でも、早期死亡のリスクをかなり下げることに関係していた**」より、空欄(ロ)を含む文は、「**強度に関係なく、**身体活動全体のレベルがより高く、座っている時間がより少なくなることが、早期死亡のリスクがより低くなることと関連している」から、**(d) regardless of**が正解。

（ハ）

(a) 有益な　(b) 診断の　(c) 広い　(d) 有害な

空欄(ハ)を含む文は、**The clinical message「臨床（病人の観察、治療を行うこと）のメッセージ」**で、**every step counts and even light activity is (　ハ　).「どの（強度の）段階も重要で、軽度の運動でも（　ハ　）」**となる。**evenは極端な具体例の目印**であり、ここでは**どの（強度の）段階も重要な具体例**なので、(ハ)には、**(a) beneficial**が入る。

論理 POINT ❷ evenは極端な具体例の目印

evenは具体例の目印になり、中でも**極端な具体例**を表します。例文をご覧ください。

（例文）

Even children can understand it.

訳 子供ですらそれを理解できる。

この例文では、**理解力が最も劣る具体例**として、「子供」が挙げられています。

（二）

(a) 豊かで　(b) 陽気で

(c) 自立して　(d) 責任を持って

空欄(二)を含む文の前半は、If we want to be healthy and (　二　) when we grow older,「もし私たちが年を取った時に健康で(　二　)いたいなら」である。**一般的に加齢に伴っておとずれるのは、貧乏や陰鬱になることや無責任になることではない**ので、(a), (b), (d)を正解の候補から外す。**(c) independent**なら、**一般的に加齢に伴って介助の手が必要になる**ので、正解となる。

設問 4.

「たとえ～しても」は**even if** ～で表し、副詞節を作る。**「座っていることが、立っていることや歩いていることによって中断されて」**は、**sitting was broken up by standing and walking**とする。**break up**で「**中断する**」の意味。主節は「そのリスクは残った」なので、The risk remained.とする。まとめると、**The risk remained, even if sitting was broken up by standing and walking.**が正解。

構文図解

Sitting still for nine and a half hours a day raises the risk of early death, a study has found.

動名詞Sitting ～ dayまでがSのカタマリ　O　S　V

Middle-aged and older people who live sedentary lives are up to two and a half times more likely to die early, researchers said. The risk remained, [even if sitting was broken up by standing and walking].

O　be ～ times more likely to do「―する可能性が～倍高い」　S　V　S　V　M

Light activity (such as cooking or washing-up) could help lessen the risk. People (who did regular physical activity of any intensity) were about five times less likely to die early [than those who were not physically active].

help do「～するのに役立つ」　S　M　V　O　S　M　V　M

The study, (in The BMJ), analysed existing research (on physical activity and mortality) [in nearly 36,400 adults aged 40 and older]. Participants had an average age (of 62) and were followed [for an average of just under six years, during which time 2,149 died].

S　M　V　O　M　M　分詞の後置修飾　S　V　O　M　V　M

Their activity levels were monitored [at the start of the research] [using devices that track physical movements] and were categorised [into "light intensity" such as slow walking, "moderate activity" such as brisk walking, vacuuming or mowing the lawn and "vigorous activity" such as jogging or digging].

S　V　M　分詞構文　M　関係代名詞のthat　V　M　"light intensity" ～ , "moderate activity" ～ , "vigorous activity" ～の3つの接続

本文訳

研究によって、1日に9時間半じっと座っていることは、早期死亡のリスクを高めることがわかった。

座ってばかりの生活を送っている中年の人、そしてそれより高齢の人は、2.5倍にまで早期死亡する可能性が高くなると、研究者は言った。たとえ座っていることが、立っていることや歩いていることによって中断されたとしても、そのリスクは残った。

料理や食器洗いのような軽い活動は、そのリスクを減らす助けとなる可能性がある。どんな強度でも、定期的に運動をする人は、身体的に活動的ではない人よりも、およそ5倍早期死亡する可能性が低くなった。

BMJ（ブリティッシュ・メディカル・ジャーナル）の研究は、40歳以上のおよそ36,400人の成人の、身体活動と死亡率の既存の研究を分析した。被験者は平均年齢が62歳で、平均すると6年弱追跡調査されて、その間に2,149人が亡くなった。

彼らの活動レベルは、体の動きを追跡する装置を使って、研究の始めから監視され、ゆっくり歩くような「軽度」、きびきび歩いたり、掃除機をかけたり、芝を刈ったりするような「中程度の活動」、そしてジョギングや穴掘りのような「精力的な活動」に分類された。

語彙リスト

still	副 じっと	monitor	動 監視する
sedentary	形 いつも座っている	device	名 装置
up to	熟 ～まで	track	動 追跡する
break up	熟 中断する	categorize A into B	熟 AをBに分類する
washing-up	名 食器洗い	moderate	形 中程度の
help do	熟 ～するのに役立つ	brisk	形 きびきびした
lessen	動 少なくする	vacuum	動 掃除機をかける
intensity	名 強度	mow	動 刈る
existing	形 既存の	lawn	名 芝
mortality	名 死亡率	vigorous	形 精力的な
participant	名 被験者	dig	動 穴を掘る

▶単語10回CHECK 1 2 3 4 5 6 7 8 9 10

構文図解

[After adjusting for potential influencing factors], researchers found 〈that any level of physical activity was associated with a substantially lower risk of early death〉.

M S V 名詞節のthat O

Deaths fell steeply [as total activity increased], [before levelling off]. People (who did light intensity activity for about five hours a day, or moderate to vigorous activity for 24 minutes a day) had the most health benefits.

S V M 比例のas M M S M from A to B「AからBまで」のfromの省略 V O

There were approximately five times as many deaths (among the 25 per cent of least active people) [compared with the 25 per cent most active].

M V M S M 分詞構文 M

Researchers looked separately [at sedentary behaviour] and found 〈sitting still for nine and a half hours or more was linked to a higher risk of early death〉. The most sedentary people, (who spent an average of nearly ten hours a day sitting), were [at a 163 per cent higher risk of dying] [before they might have been expected to] [during the period of the study] [than the least sedentary, who sat for an average of seven and a half hours].

S V M M V 名詞節のthatの省略 O S M spend O doingのdoing V M the most sedentary peopleを指す M dieの省略 M M

本文訳

影響を与える可能性のある要因を調整した後で、研究者は、どんなレベルの身体活動でも、早期死亡のリスクをかなり下げることに関係しているということを見出した。

死亡数は、全体の活動が増えるにつれて急落し、その後、横ばいになった。1日につきおよそ5時間の軽度の活動、あるいは1日につき中程度から精力的な運動を24分間行う人は、最も高い健康効果を得られた。

最も活動的な25%の人と比べると、最も活動的ではない25%の人の中で、およそ5倍の人が亡くなった。

研究者は、座っている行為を単独で見て、9時間半かそれ以上じっと座っていることは、早期死亡のより高いリスクとつながっているとわかった。最も長く座っている人は、1日平均10時間座っているが、平均して7時間半と最も座っている時間が少ない人に比べて、その研究期間中、寿命より若くして死ぬリスクが163%高かった。

語彙リスト

□ be associated with	熟	～に関連する
□ substantially	副	かなり
□ level off	熟	横ばいになる
□ approximately	副	およそ
□ separately	副	単独で

▶単語10回CHECK 1 □ 2 □ 3 □ 4 □ 5 □ 6 □ 7 □ 8 □ 9 □ 10 □

構文図解

Ulf Ekelund, (of the Norwegian School of Sport Sciences in Oslo),
S M
(who led the research), said: “Our findings provide clear scientific
M V S V O
evidence 〈that higher levels of total physical activity, regardless of
同格のthat M
intensity, and less sedentary time are associated with lower risk of
premature mortality in middle-aged and older people〉.”

Researchers (from Germany and New Zealand) said 〈that the
S M V 名詞節のthat
study was an important addition to existing knowledge but could not
O
explain whether the distribution of activity across the day or week
名詞節のwhether「〜かどうか」
was relevant〉.

Researchersを指す
They added: “The clinical message seems straightforward: every
S V S V C S
step counts and even light activity is beneficial.”
V S V C

[Commenting on the research], Jess Kuehne, (of the Centre for
分詞構文 M S M
Ageing Better), said: “ [If we want to be healthy and independent
V M
when we grow older], we need to do much more [in our forties and
S V O M
fifties]. [As well as aerobic exercise like taking brisk walks, cycling
M 前置詞のlike
or swimming], we also need to be boosting the strength (in our
S M V O M
muscles and bones) and improving our balance.
boostingとimprovingの接続 V O

本文訳

その研究を行ったオスロにあるノルウェースポーツサイエンス校のウルフ・エケルンドはこう言った。「我々の研究結果は、強度に関係なく、身体活動全体のレベルがより高く、座っている時間がより少なくなることが、中高年で早期死亡のリスクがより低くなることと関連している、という明らかな科学的証拠を与えている」。

ドイツやニュージーランドの研究者は、その研究は既存の知識に重要なことを加えたが、1日、あるいは1週間での活動の配分が関係しているかどうかを説明できていないと言った。

彼らはこう続けた。「その臨床のメッセージは単純なように思える。すなわち、どの（強度の）段階も重要で、軽度の活動でも有益である」

その研究について意見を述べ、エイジングベターセンターのジェス・キューネはこう言った。「もし私たちが年を取った時に健康で自立していたいなら、40代、50代でもっと多くのことをやる必要がある。きびきび歩く、サイクリング、スイミングのような有酸素運動だけでなく、私たちは筋肉や骨の強度を高めて、バランスを改善する必要がある。

語彙リスト

premature	形	早すぎる
mortality	名	死
addition	名	追加
distribution	名	分配
relevant	形	関連している
clinical	形	臨床の
straightforward	形	単純な
count	動	重要だ
comment on	動	～について意見を述べる
aerobic	形	有酸素性の
boost	動	高める

▸単語10回CHECK 1 2 3 4 5 6 7 8 9 10

構文図解

運動すること全般を指す

It's [not just about adding years to our life], it's [about adding life to our years and increasing the time that we stay fit, healthy and free from long-term health conditions or disability]."

S V (It's) / M [not just about adding years to our life] / S V (it's) / M [about adding life to ... disability]

関係副詞の that

adding life ~ years と increasing ~ disability の接続

fit, healthy, free の3つの接続

本文訳

それは、単に私たちの人生に寿命を加えてくれるだけでなく、私たちの寿命に活力を加えてくれるもので、私たちが元気で健康で、長期間の健康状態や身体障害の心配から解放される時間を増やしてくれる」。

語彙リスト

fit	形	元気な
free from	熟	～から免れて
disability	名	身体障害

▶単語10回CHECK 1 2 3 4 5 6 7 8 9 10

Sitting still for nine and a half hours a day raises the risk of early death, a study has found.

Middle-aged and older people who live sedentary lives are up to two and a half times more likely to die early, researchers said. The risk remained, even if sitting was broken up by standing and walking.

Light activity such as cooking or washing-up could help lessen the risk. People who did regular physical activity of any intensity were about five times less likely to die early than those who were not physically active.

The study, in The BMJ, analysed existing research on physical activity and mortality in nearly 36,400 adults aged 40 and older. Participants had an average age of 62 and were followed for an average of just under six years, during which time 2,149 died.

Their activity levels were monitored at the start of the research using devices that track physical movements and were categorised into "light intensity" such as slow walking, "moderate activity" such as brisk walking, vacuuming or mowing the lawn and "vigorous activity" such as jogging or digging.

After adjusting for potential influencing factors, researchers found that any level of physical activity was associated with a substantially lower risk of early death.

Deaths fell steeply as total activity increased, before levelling off. People who did light intensity activity for about five hours a day, or moderate to vigorous activity for 24 minutes a day had the most health benefits.

There were approximately five times as many deaths among the 25 per cent of least active people compared with the 25 per cent most active.

Researchers looked separately at sedentary behaviour and found sitting still for nine and a half hours or more was linked to a higher risk of early death. The most sedentary people, who spent an average of nearly ten hours a day sitting, were at a 163 per cent higher risk of dying before they might have been expected to during the period of the study than the least sedentary, who sat for an average of seven and a half hours.

Ulf Ekelund, of the Norwegian School of Sport Sciences in Oslo, who led the research, said: "Our findings provide clear scientific evidence that higher levels of total physical activity, regardless of intensity, and less sedentary time are associated with lower risk of premature mortality in middle-aged and older people."

Researchers from Germany and New Zealand said that the study was an important addition to existing knowledge but could not explain whether the distribution of activity across the day or week was relevant.

They added: "The clinical message seems straightforward: every step counts and even light activity is beneficial."

Commenting on the research, Jess Kuehne, of the Centre for Ageing Better, said: "If we want to be healthy and independent when we grow older, we need to do much more in our forties and fifties. As well as aerobic exercise like taking brisk walks, cycling or swimming, we also need to be boosting the strength in our muscles and bones and improving our balance. It's not just about adding years to our life, it's about adding life to our years and increasing the time that we stay fit, healthy and free from long-term health conditions or disability."

▸音読10回CHECK 1 2 3 4 5 6 7 8 9 10

背景知識が広がるコラム

BACKGROUND KNOWLEDGE

椅子に座ることの弊害とその対策

私自身が受験生の頃は、『勉強しすぎて死んだ者はいない、だから頑張れ』なんていう、今となっては暴論とも言うべき励ましが横行していた気がします。本問を読んでわかったように、**椅子に座る時間が長いほど、健康に深刻なマイナスの影響**があります。勉強は、基本は椅子に座って行うものなので、勉強し続けることは、実は体に相当な負担を課す作業でもあります。

実際、家にこもって勉強をし続けると、あっという間に体重が増えて、健康に悪影響を与えるのがわかるでしょう。ただ、勉強が将来の道を開いてくれるのも間違いのないことです。そこで、**椅子に座る弊害をどう軽減するか**が重要になります。

本文にも登場したように、やはり運動がカギを握っています。運動はジョギング、サイクリング、ウォーキングに代表される**有酸素運動**と、筋トレに代表される**無酸素運動**、そして**ストレッチ**に大別できます。これを時間帯と自分の体力によって、上手に組み合わせることをおすすめします。

まずは、最も負荷が軽く、かつ簡単に始められるストレッチを、夜寝る前、あるいは風呂上がりに行うのがおすすめです。これにより、わずかな効果ですが、椅子に座る弊害を軽減できます。

続いて、**筋トレ**を**午前中、あるいは夕方**に、**スクワット**、**腕立て伏せ**などをやるとよいでしょう。夜に行うと身体が覚醒して不眠につながる恐れがあるので注意しましょう。特に、**椅子に座り続けて悪くなった血流を良くするには、スクワットがおすすめ**です。

最後に、**手軽で長時間できるウォーキング**は、最もおすすめです。朝食の前後、昼食の前後、夕食後など、そして勉強に飽きたら、とにもかくにもウォーキングをすることをおすすめします。私自身も、椅子に座って本書の執筆をしていますが、バランスをとるために、ウォーキングをこまめに行い、筋トレも必ず定期的に行うことで、体のバランスを整えています。

問題 6

文化

イギリス人と犬の関係

別冊 p.24 ／制限時間 25 分／ 546 words

解答

設問(1) SPCA が王立協会になった名誉のこと。

設問(2) イギリス人は、人間といるより動物といるほうが、自由に自分を表現できるように思えること。

設問(3) 「最悪だった」というような、否定的な意味。

設問(4) イギリスでは、犬は少なくとも 19 世紀までは軽蔑され、ときに虐待されてきたという事実と、現代では犬は最愛の仲間とみなされ、大きな愛情をもって扱われているという事実。

設問(5) 家で待っている犬が、飼い主がオフィスを出発して、家に向かって移動し始める瞬間を知っているという能力。

設問(6) a British dog's life

設問(7) 犬を好きになると、その飼い主も好きになること。

設問(8) （ i ）ロ　（ii）ハ　（iii）ニ　（iv）ロ

解説

設問(1)

(a) **that honor**「**その名誉**」から、これより前の部分で名誉となる内容を探す。すると、この文の前半に **the SPCA went on to become the Royal Society（RSPCA）**とあるので、「**SPCA が王立協会になった名誉のこと**」が正解。**go on to do**「**続けて〜する**」の熟語に注意する。

設問(2)

下線部(b) **this aspect**「**この側面**」には、**of the Brits' relationship with their pets**「**イギリス人のペットとの関係**」という修飾語が付いているので、**これより前にイギリス人とペットとの関係を記した部分**があると判断する。それは、この前文 **we seem more able to freely express ourselves with animals than we are with other people.**「**私たち（イギリス人）は、人間といるより動物といるほうが、自由に自**

分を表現できるように思える」なので、これが正解となる。

設問(3)

下線部(c)の前文dogs were treated **with contempt and sometimes cruelty**.「犬は**軽蔑されて、ときに虐待されてきた**」や、下線部(c)の次の文**No positive qualities**「**まったくプラスの性質はない**」をヒントにする。すると、質問は"What was it like?"「それはどんな感じだった？」なので、答えの**An absolute dog!**は、「**最悪だったよ！**」というような、否定的な意味を表していることになる。

設問(4)

下線部(d)を含む文は、～, the modern reality is that **the British treat dogs with huge affection, looking on them as beloved companions and having lifelong bonds with them.**「現代の現実は、**イギリス人は犬を最愛の仲間とみなして生涯の絆を結び、大きな愛情を持って扱っている**ということだ」である。

それと正反対の内容が、下線部(d)の前（第3段落第5文）にある**dogs were treated with contempt and sometimes cruelty**.「**犬は軽蔑されて、ときに虐待されてきた**」や、同段落第4文,our language is crammed with phrases suggesting that **a dog's life, at least up to the nineteenth century, was a miserable fate**「**私たちの言語には少なくとも19世紀までは、犬の生涯が惨めな運命だった**ことを示す表現でいっぱいだ」である。

以上をまとめると、「**イギリスでは、犬は少なくとも19世紀までは軽蔑され、ときに虐待されてきたという事実と、現代では犬は最愛の仲間とみなされ、大きな愛情を持って扱われているという事実**」が正解となる。

設問(5)

下線部(e)の次の文に、for exampleがあり、その後で具体化されている。**dogs waiting at home know the moment their owners leave the office and begin their homeward journey**「**家で待っている犬が、飼い主がオフィスを出発して、家に向かって移動し始める瞬間を知っている**」という**能力**が正解。

設問(6)

下線部(f)を含む文は、the sense of (f) the phrase has gradually changed and now means **to have a cosseted and comfortable existence**「その言葉の意味が次第に変わってきて、今や逆に、**甘やかされて心地良い暮らしをする**ことを意味すると考える批評家もいる」から、**犬に関する表現**とわかる。そこから前文の**a British dog's life**が正解となる。

設問(7)

itは前文の**Love my dog, love me.「私の犬が好きなら、私も愛して」**という表現を指すとわかるので、**犬を好きになると、その飼い主も好きになること**が正解。

設問(8)

(ⅰ) 根気強さ
(イ) 友情　(ロ) 粘り強さ
(ハ) 適切さ　(ニ) 野生

doggednessは「**根気強さ**」を意味するので、最も近い**(ロ) persistence「粘り強さ」**が正解。

(ⅱ) ～に調和した
(イ) ～が原因の　(ロ) ～と相互関係のある
(ハ) ～と調和して　(ニ) ～に服従して

下線部(ⅱ)を含む文の次の文は、「家で待っている犬が飼い主がオフィスを出て家路につく瞬間がわかる」という、**犬と飼い主が通じ合っている例**なので「**～と調和して**」の意味の**(ハ) in harmony with**が正解。**be attuned to「～に調和する」**の意味の熟語。

(ⅲ) 証明されて
(イ) 運ばれて　(ロ) 修正されて
(ハ) 産み出されて　(ニ) 裏付けられて

bear out「～を証明する」から、**(ニ) supported「裏付けられて」**が正解。

下線部(ⅲ)を含む文は、this cozy impression is not (ⅲ) borne out by our behavior in the real world.「この心地よい印象は、実世界の私たちの行動によって (ⅲ) borne outされていない」となる。this cozy impressionとは、前の段落の「**イギリスでの犬の暮らしが、甘やかされ**

て心地良い暮らしへと変わった」ことを意味する。

下線部(ⅲ)を含む文の次の文で、「**捨て犬の数がたくさんいる**」ことから（ニ）supportedを選んで、「**犬を大事にする印象は私たちの行動で裏付けられていない**」＝「**犬を大事にする印象に、私たちの行動が伴っているわけではない**」となる。

(ⅳ)　発生率
（イ）　事件　　（ロ）　数
（ハ）　場合　　（ニ）　再発

下線部(ⅳ)を含む文は、the (ⅳ) incidence of stray and abandoned dogs in England was estimated at around 111,000.「イングランドの捨て犬、野良犬の (ⅳ) incidenceは、およそ11万1千件と見積もられていた」となる。「**11万1千件**」からも **(ⅳ)は「数」を意味するとわかる**ので、**（ロ）number**が正解。**(ⅳ) incidence**は「**発生率**」の意味。incidentなら「事件」の意味なので、（イ）accidentと同義になる。incidenceとincidentは混同しやすいので注意する。

構文図解

Everyone knows 〈that we Brits treat our dogs better than our
S V 名詞節のthat O
children〉, and we are often reminded 〈that the Society for the
S V remind O that 〜の受動態のthat O
Prevention of Cruelty to Animals (SPCA) was founded in 1824, sixty
years before the National Society for the Prevention of Cruelty to
形式主語のit 名詞節のthat
Children〉. Is it deeply meaningful 〈that the SPCA went on to become
V S C S′
the Royal Society (RSPCA) while the children's society still waits for
that honor〉?
SPCAがRSPCAになる栄誉のこと

What, then, lies [behind this remarkable but apparently sincere
S M V M
The truth is that 〜. と同じ表現
attachment we have to our dogs]? The truth is, we seem more able to
関係詞の省略 S V S V C
freely express ourselves with animals [than we are with other people].
M able to express ourselvesの省略
Kate Fox, the British social commentator, [pondering on this aspect
S S′ 分詞構文 M
of the Brits' relationship with their pets], explains convincingly,
V M
"unlike our fellow Englishmen, animals are not embarrassed or put
O
off by our un-English displays of emotion."

The word dog itself is peculiarly native [to Britain] and comes
S V C M V
[from an obscure Old English past]. The alternative Germanic term,
M S hunting dogsを指す
hound, refers mainly to 〈hunting dogs〉. [In feudal society], such dogs
S′ V O M S
might be given special treatment [by their lordly master] and be fed
V O M V
[from his table].
M their lordly masterを指す

本文訳

私たちイギリス人が、犬を自分の子供よりも大切に扱うことはみんなが知っているし、私たちは、動物虐待防止協会（SPCA）が、国立児童虐待防止協会よりも60年早い1824年に設立されたことをよく思い出す。SPCAが、王立協会（RSPCA）に昇格している一方で、児童のための協会がまだその名誉を待っているということには、深い意味があるのではないか？

そして、私たちの犬にかけるこの異常だが明らかに真剣な愛情の背後には何があるのか？　実は、私たちは、人間といるより動物といるほうが、自由に自分を表現できるように思える。イギリスの社会批評家であるケイト・フォックスは、イギリス人のペットとの関係のこの側面を熟慮して、「私たちの仲間の英国人と違って、動物は私たちの英国人らしからぬ感情表現に困惑したり、うんざりしたりしない」と納得のいく説明をする。

dogという単語それ自体は、イギリス生まれの独特なもので、はっきりしない昔の古英語から来ている。代わりとなるゲルマン語系の用語のhoundは、主に狩猟犬について言うものだ。*封建社会では、そのような犬は貴族の飼い主に特別扱いされて、飼い主の食卓でえさを与えられていたかもしれない。

*「封建社会」は、中世社会の基本的な支配形態である、君主が領地を諸侯に分け与えて支配させる制度を基としている社会。

語彙リスト

Brit	名 イギリス人
prevention	名 防止
cruelty	名 虐待
found	動 設立する
go on to do	熟 続けて~する
honor	名 名誉
remarkable	形 異常な
apparently	副 明らかに
sincere	形 真剣な
attachment	名 愛情
ponder on	熟 熟慮する
aspect	名 側面
convincingly	副 納得のいくように
put off	熟 うんざりさせる
fellow	名 仲間
display	名 表現
peculiarly	副 特に
obscure	形 はっきりしない
alternative	形 代わりの
term	名 用語
refer to	熟 ~を表す
feudal	形 封建制の
treatment	名 扱い
lordly	形 貴族の
master	名 飼い主
feed	動 ~にえさを与える

▸単語10回CHECK 1 2 3 4 5 6 7 8 9 10

構文図解

狩猟犬とその他の犬の対比

But lesser dogs (out in the yard) had a rougher time, and our language is crammed [with phrases suggesting that a dog's life, at least up to the nineteenth century, was a miserable fate: dog-tired, dogsbody, going to the dogs, die like a dog, and so on]. [For the most part], dogs were treated [with contempt and sometimes cruelty]. Even the question, "What was it like?" might produce the answer, "An absolute dog!" No positive qualities here, then.

S M V O S V M M S V M S S′ V O O′ M

分詞の後置修飾　名詞節のthat

[In curious contrast], the modern reality is 〈that the British treat dogs with huge affection, looking on them as beloved companions and having lifelong bonds with them〉. The British adore the legendary image (of a dog's faithfulness and literal doggedness).

M S V C S V O M

dogsを指す　名詞節のthat　分詞構文　look on A as Bのas　looking ～とhaving ～の接続　dogsを指す

Nature seems to provide (plenty of) evidence (to justify this attitude). Endless anecdotes suggest 〈that dogs are strangely and deeply attuned to their owners, with some observers believing their pets have psychic powers〉. The researcher and scientist Rupert Sheldrake, [for example], has conducted surveys (to demonstrate that dogs (among other pets) waiting at home know the moment their owners leave the office and begin their homeward journey).

S V M O M S V O S M V O M

犬の忠誠心や根気強さのようなイメージを称賛すること　不定詞 形容詞的用法　名詞節のthat　付帯状況のwith（some observersがO、believingがC）　名詞節のthatの省略　不定詞 形容詞的用法　名詞節のthat　分詞の後置修飾　関係詞の省略

本文訳

しかし、庭の外にいる小型犬は、より過酷な時代を過ごしていて、私たちの言語には、少なくとも19世紀までは、犬の生涯が惨めな運命だったことを示す表現でいっぱいだ。例えば、dog-tired（へとへとで）、dogsbody（下っ端）、going to the dogs（堕落すること）、die like a dog（みじめな死を遂げる）などがある。ほとんどにおいて犬は軽蔑されて、ときに虐待されてきた。「それはどうでしたか？」という質問でさえ、「最悪だった！（An absolute dog!）」という返答が生じるかもしれない。ここにはまったくプラスの性質はない。

不思議なほど対照的に、現代の現実は、イギリス人は犬を最愛の仲間とみなして生涯の絆を結び、大きな愛情を持って扱っているということだ。イギリス人は、犬の忠実さや文字通りの根気強さという伝説的なイメージが大好きだ。

自然は、この態度を正当化するのに、たくさんの証拠を提供しているように思える。数えきれないほどの逸話は、犬が妙に強く飼い主に調和していて、そのペットが超能力を持っていると信じる者もいる。例えば、研究者で科学者のルパート・シェルドレークが、（他のペットの中でもとりわけ）家で待っている犬が、飼い主がオフィスを出発して、家に向かって移動し始める瞬間を知っていることを示す調査を行った。

語彙リスト

□ rough	形 過酷な	□ lifelong	形 生涯の
□ be crammed with	熟 ～で詰まっている	□ bond	名 絆
□ phrase	名 表現	□ adore	動 ～が大好きである
□ miserable	形 惨めな	□ legendary	形 伝説の
□ fate	名 運命	□ faithfulness	名 忠実さ
□ contempt	名 軽蔑	□ literal	形 文字通りの
□ absolute	形 絶対的な	□ doggedness	名 根気強さ
□ in contrast	熟 対照的に	□ justify	動 正当化する
□ huge	形 巨大な	□ anecdote	名 逸話
□ affection	名 愛情	□ be attuned to	熟 ～に調和する
□ look on A as B	熟 AをBとみなす	□ psychic	形 超能力の
□ beloved	形 最愛の	□ survey	名 調査
□ companion	名 仲間	□ homeward	形 家に向かう

▸単語10回CHECK 1 □ 2 □ 3 □ 4 □ 5 □ 6 □ 7 □ 8 □ 9 □ 10 □

構文図解

So what is a British dog's life like these days? Some commentators think 〈the sense of the phrase has gradually changed and now means to have a cosseted and comfortable existence, rather than the opposite〉. I am quite sure 〈the Queen's corgis would agree with that〉.

前置詞のlike

M V S M M S V O

名詞節のthatの省略

cosseted and comfortableと反対の意味

S V O

名詞節のthatの省略

dogという語の持つイメージがマイナスからプラスに転じたこと

However, this cozy impression is not borne out [by our behavior in the real world]. [According to a 2013 survey], the incidence 〈of stray and abandoned dogs in England〉 was estimated [at around 111,000].

M S V M

dogの持つプラスのイメージ

M S M V M

What's going on here? Two extremes of behavior meeting in a confused national psyche? It does seem [that, in their attitudes to animals and children, we find one of the paradoxes of the British temperament].

S V M

強調の助動詞do

What's going on?に対する回答

S V M

[All the same], there is one common expression 〈which continues to suggest a bond between human and animal that is more than mere friendship〉: "Love me, love my dog." Or rather, [in practice], "Love my dog, love me." Watch dog owners meeting in a public park and you will see 〈how it works〉. Better than a dating agency any time.

M M V S M

関係代名詞のthat（先行詞はa bond）

V O V O M M

V O V O V O C

S V O

単なる友情を越えた人間と犬の絆

本文訳

では、最近のイギリスの犬の暮らしはどのようなものか？　その表現の意味が次第に変わってきて、今や逆に、甘やかされて心地よい暮らしをすることを意味すると考える批評家もいる。私は女王のコーギー犬ならそれに同意するだろうと、確信している。

しかし、この心地よい印象に、実世界の私たちの行動が伴っているわけではない。2013年の調査によると、イングランドの野良犬、捨て犬の発生率は、およそ11万1千件と見積もられた。

この地で何が起きているのか？　両極端な行動が、混乱した国民の精神の中でぶつかっているのか？　動物や子供への態度に、私たちは、実はイギリス人の気質の矛盾の1つを見出せるように思える。

にもかかわらず、人間と動物の単なる友情を越えた絆を示し続ける1つの共通の表現がある。「私が好きなら、私の犬も愛して」だ。あるいはむしろ、実際は「私の犬が好きなら私も愛して」だ。犬の飼い主同士が公園で会っているところを観察すれば、それがどう機能しているかがわかるだろう。どんなときでも、交際相手紹介所よりもうまくいっている。

語彙リスト

cosset	動 ～を甘やかす
opposite	名 反対のこと
cozy	形 気持ちの良い
bear out	熟 証明する
incidence	名 発生率
stray	形 家のない
abandon	動 捨てる
estimate	動 見積もる
extreme	名 極端なこと
psyche	名 精神
paradox	名 矛盾
temperament	名 気質
all the same	熟 にもかかわらず
in practice	熟 実際は
dating agency	名 交際相手紹介所

▶単語10回CHECK　1　2　3　4　5　6　7　8　9　10

Everyone knows that we Brits treat our dogs better than our children, and we are often reminded that the Society for the Prevention of Cruelty to Animals (SPCA) was founded in 1824, sixty years before the National Society for the Prevention of Cruelty to Children. Is it deeply meaningful that the SPCA went on to become the Royal Society (RSPCA) while the children's society still waits for that honor?

What, then, lies behind this remarkable but apparently sincere attachment we have to our dogs? The truth is, we seem more able to freely express ourselves with animals than we are with other people. Kate Fox, the British social commentator, pondering on this aspect of the Brits' relationship with their pets, explains convincingly, "unlike our fellow Englishmen, animals are not embarrassed or put off by our un-English displays of emotion."

The word dog itself is peculiarly native to Britain and comes from an obscure Old English past. The alternative Germanic term, hound, refers mainly to hunting dogs. In feudal society, such dogs might be given special treatment by their lordly master and be fed from his table. But lesser dogs out in the yard had a rougher time, and our language is crammed with phrases suggesting that a dog's life, at least up to the nineteenth century, was a miserable fate: dog-tired, dogsbody, going to the dogs, die like a dog, and so on. For the most part, dogs were treated with contempt and sometimes cruelty. Even the question, "What was it like?" might produce the answer, "An absolute dog!" No positive qualities here, then.

In curious contrast, the modern reality is that the British treat dogs with huge affection, looking on them as beloved companions and having lifelong bonds with them. The British adore the legendary image of a dog's faithfulness and literal doggedness.

Nature seems to provide plenty of evidence to justify this attitude. Endless anecdotes suggest that dogs are strangely and deeply attuned to their owners, with some observers believing their pets have psychic powers. The researcher and scientist Rupert Sheldrake, for example, has conducted surveys to demonstrate that dogs (among other pets) waiting at home know the moment their owners leave the office and begin their homeward journey.

So what is a British dog's life like these days? Some commentators think the sense of the phrase has gradually changed and now means to have a cosseted and comfortable existence, rather than the opposite. I am quite sure the Queen's corgis would agree with that.

However, this cozy impression is not borne out by our behavior in the real world. According to a 2013 survey, the incidence of stray and abandoned dogs in England was estimated at around 111,000.

What's going on here? Two extremes of behavior meeting in a confused national psyche? It does seem that, in their attitudes to animals and children, we find one of the paradoxes of the British temperament.

All the same, there is one common expression which continues to suggest a bond between human and animal that is more than mere friendship: "Love me, love my dog." Or rather, in practice, "Love my dog, love me." Watch dog owners meeting in a public park and you will see how it works. Better than a dating agency any time.

▸音読10回CHECK 1 2 3 4 5 6 7 8 9 10

背景知識が広がるコラム

BACKGROUND KNOWLEDGE

人間と犬・猫の関係性の歴史

犬は猫と並んで、人間にペットとして飼われることの多い動物ですが、歴史上は**犬のほうが先に人間と生活を共にし始めた**ようです。

太古の昔、**狩猟の際に獲物を捕まえたり、追いかけさせたりするために、犬を家畜化した**と考えられています。人間よりもはるかに走るのが速く、小回りが効くので、狩りにおいて非常に重宝したようです。

一方で、**猫が家畜化**されたのは、**穀物を栽培する生活になってから**です。元々は、**穀物を食い荒らすネズミを退治するため**に、猫を飼うようになったと考えられています。**狩猟・採集の時代に犬は家畜化**されて、**穀物を栽培して定住する生活になってから猫が家畜化**されたようです。

初めは家畜として利用されてきた犬ですが、次第に**ペットとして飼われる**ようになりました。**古代エジプトの神話**には「**アヌビス神**」という犬の姿をした神が登場しており、犬は神聖なものと崇拝されていたようです。『**日本書紀**』にも**犬は神として登場**することから、日本においても、犬が神格化されていた時代があったようです。一方、古代エジプトで愛と美の女神は「**バステト神**」といい、**人間の体に猫の頭という姿**をしており、愛と豊穣を司る神として、崇拝されていました。

その後、**犬も猫も、時代によって崇拝されたり迫害されたりと、人間の信仰によって、様々な扱いを受けてきた**ようです。

問題 7

学問

人文科学の危機

別冊 p.28 ／制限時間 25 分／ 555 words

解答

[1] ① 1　② 4　③ 2　④ 2
[2] (1) 1　(2) 2　(3) 2　(4) 3
[3] 3, 6　[4] (A) 5　(B) 1
[5] 3　[6] 3, 4, 6

解説

[1]

① 1. 重大な　2. 小さい　3. 元気のよい　4. 卑劣な

下線部①**grave**は「**重大な**」の意味なので、**1. serious**が正解。「**重大な**」のパラフレーズは頻出なので、以下にまとめる。

語彙 POINT ⑤ 「重大な」のパラフレーズ

important ／ significant ／ serious ／ grave ／ critical

「**重大な**」で**一番よく使われる単語が important**です。**significant は important を少し堅くした言葉**です。**serious**には「**深刻で真剣に対処すべき**」というニュアンスがあり、**grave**は「**非常に深刻な**」、**critical**は「**非常に重要な**」というニュアンスがあります。

② 1. 明るい　2. 運命にある
　3. 希望にあふれている　4. 不確実だ

下線部②**hangs in the balance**は直訳の「**バランスを取ってぶら下がっている**」から、「**不安定な状態にある**」、「**未解決のままである**」となるので、**4. is uncertain**が正解。**hang in the air**も「**空中でぶら下がっている**」＝「**不安定な状態だ**」、「**未解決のままだ**」を表す。

③ 1. 基礎　2. 発達　3. 判断　4. 支払い

下線部③**cultivation**は**畑などを対象**とすると「**耕作**」の意味だが、**才能や技術などを対象**とすると「**育成**」の意味になるので、**2. development**が一番近い意味で正解となる。

④ 1. 軍事的優位性を求めての競争
2. お金や権力を求めての競争
3. 学生を勝たせるための競争
4. 票を獲得するための競争

下線部④のthe competitive flurryは、直訳すると「**競争の混乱**」だが、何を求めて競争するかがわからないので、文脈で考える。下線部④を含む文は、other abilities, equally crucial, are **at risk of getting lost** in ④the competitive flurry, である。第5段落最終文に、**With the rush to profitability** in the global market, values precious for the future of democracy, ～, **are in danger of getting lost**.「世界市場で**利益追求に殺到する**中、民主主義の将来に貴重な価値観が失われつつある」とあり、これが同義と判断できればmoneyが使われている**2. The race for money and power**が正解とわかる。

> **解法 POINT ❸ 同形反復**
>
> 英文では、**同じ形が反復されると、同じ意味か反対の意味**になることがあります。この視点で解答を導けることがよくあるので、同じ形の反復には注意を払いましょう。

本問でも、第5段落最終文の**are in danger of getting lost**と下線部④の文の**are at risk of getting lostが同じ形で同じ意味**、かつ**第5段落最終文values precious for the future of democracy**と下線部④の文の**abilities crucial to the health of any democracy**が同じ形なので、2つの文の類似点に気付くことで解答を導ける。

[2]

(1) 1. 近くに　2. せいぜい　3. 正午　4. すぐに

空欄(1)を含む文は、everyone knew that a crisis was at (1), and many world leaders **worked quickly and desperately to find solutions.**「すべての人が危機は(1)と知り、世界のリーダーの多くが、**素早く必死になって解決策を探ろうと努めた**」から、「**危機が身近に迫っている**」とわかるので**1. hand**が正解。**at hand**「**近くに**」の意味

の熟語。

(2) 1. 頼む　2. 提起された　3. 取り換えられた　4. 声

空欄(2)を含む部分は、too few questions have been (2) about the direction of educationなので、「教育の方向性に関して、あまりに少ない疑問しか(2)されなかった」と**受動態を作る**ことになり、② posedか③replacedに正解の候補を絞る。「**疑問が提起される**」という**主語と述語の対応**から、② **posed**が正解。

(3) 1. 訂正　2. 異論　3. 拒絶　4. 提案

空欄(3)を含む文の前文に、**science and technology are of crucial importance** for the future health of their nations「**自然科学や科学技術は、**彼らの国家の健全な将来に**極めて重要だ**」とある。それには「私たちは、**優れた自然科学や科学技術の教育に異論はないはずだ**」と続くのが自然で、**2. objectionが正解**となる。3. rejectionは言い過ぎの選択肢で不適。

(4) 1. 無視できるほどの　2. 汚染　3. 緊急の　4. 些細な

空欄(4)はproblemsを修飾しており、**人文科学の危機**は、**第1段落第3文**で「**身近に迫っている**」、**第4段落第1文This crisis is facing us**「**この危機は私たちの目の前にある**」からも、**急を要する問題とわかる**ので、**3. pressing**が正解。

[3]

1. すべて　2. ～を考慮すると　3. 成長
4. とても熱心に　5. 国々　6. ～によって求められた
7. 経済の

空欄(X)を含む文は、(X), especially ～, too few questions have been (2)となるので、主節のtoo few questions have been (2)に対する**副詞節を予測**する。すると、2.と7.を使って、**given that ～「～を考慮すると」**が完成する。～には、**economic growth is so eagerly sought by all nations「経済成長がすべての国家によってとても熱心に追及されている」**と並び換えると文脈も通るので、完成。番号を当てはめると、**2-7-3-4-6-1-5**となり、**3番目は3、5番目は6**が正解。

[4]

1. ～について　2. ～で　3. それに加えて
4. しかしながら　5. ～のような　6. さらに
7. それ　8. その後すぐに

空欄(A)を含む文は、No, I mean **a crisis that goes largely unnoticed,** (　A　) a cancerである。**「ほとんど気付かれずに進行する危機」の具体例がcancer「ガン」**なので、**具体例を示す前置詞のlikeが入る**。よって、**5. like**が正解。

空欄(B)を含む文は、We haven't really thought hard (　B　) these changesである。hardをいったん読み飛ばすと、**think about「～について考える」**が使われているとわかるので、**1. about**が正解。

[5]

1. 偽物の危機　2. 財政危機
3. 静かな危機　4. 目に見える危機

第1段落最終文 a worldwide crisis in education「世界的な教育の危機」から、2. The Financial Crisisは不適。同文の**a crisis that goes largely unnoticed「ほとんど気付かれずに進行する危機」**から、**3. The Silent Crisis**が正解。

[6]

1. 世界中の教育制度に起きている根本的な変化は、徹底した考慮の結果だ。
2. 私たちは、自然科学を切り捨てて、人文科学と芸術にもっと資源を投資するべきだ。
3. 教育から人文科学と芸術を削減することは、健全な民主国家に有害な影響を与える可能性がある。
4. 他人の立場になって考えられることは、人文科学と芸術につながりのある重要な技術だ。
5. 人文科学と芸術は切り捨てられているが、学生はその重要性を十分に認識している。
6. 2008年に始まった世界規模での経済危機があった。
7. 地方の伝統は望ましくないもので、越えていくべきものだ。
8. 現代国家は、収益性をあまり重視していない傾向にある。

第３段落第２文 **The humanities and the arts are being cut away**「**人文科学と芸術が切り捨てられている**」から、**本問の危機とは人文科学と芸術の軽視**にあるとわかる。続いて**第6段落第3文**other abilities, equally crucial, are at risk of getting lost in the competitive flurry, **abilities crucial to the health of any democracy internally**「他の能力、すなわち、**どんな民主国家でもその内部の健全さにとって不可欠の能力**だが、競争の混乱の中で損なわれる危機に瀕している」より、**他の能力とは、人文科学と芸術の勉強により身に付くもの**なので、**3. Cutting the humanities and arts from education is likely to have harmful consequences for the health of democracies.**が正解。

最終段落第１文 **These abilities are associated with the humanities and the arts**「**次に述べる能力は、人文科学と芸術に関連している**」と、**同文の最後the ability to imagine sympathetically the predicaments of another person**「**他人の苦境を共感して想像する能力**」から、**4. Being able to put your feet in other people's shoes is a key skill connected with the humanities and arts.**が正解。**put one's feet in other people's shoes**「**他人の気持ちになって考える**」の熟語に注意する。

論理 POINT ③ 後方照応のthese

theseは通常**前方照応**といって、前に出てきた具体的記述をまとめる役割がありますが、例外的に**後方照応**といって、具体例が後ろに続く使い方もあります。例文をご覧ください。
（例文）
On the blackboard **these words** were written: Reading, Writing, Speaking, Listening.
訳 黒板に、**次に述べる言葉**が書かれていた。読み、書き、話す、聞くこと。

例文では、**these words** の具体例が Reading, Writing, Speaking, Listeningになるので、「**次に述べる言葉**」と訳します。

第１段落第２文No, I do not mean the global economic crisis that began in 2008.「**私は2008年に始まった世界的な経済危機を意味しているのではない**」より、**6. There was a worldwide economic**

crisis which started in 2008. が正解となる。

不正解の選択肢を見ていくと、1. は**第2段落第1文後半these changes have not been well thought through.「こうした変化はよく考え抜かれてはいない」**と反するので不適。2.は、**第6段落第2文 We should have no objection to good scientific and technical education「私たちは、優れた自然科学や科学技術の教育に対しての異論はないはずだ」**に反するので不適。

5.は、前半のThe humanities and arts are being cut away, までは正しいが、but以下に問題がある。**第3段落第3文後半** they are rapidly losing their place in curricula, and also **in the minds and hearts of parents and children「それら（人文科学や芸術）は、**カリキュラムや、同様に**親や子供の頭や心の中で急速に居場所を失いつつある**」に反するので不適。

解法 POINT ④ 選択肢を切って考える

これは誤りの選択肢を作る際によく使われる技術で、**副詞節は正しいけれど、主節が間違っている**、あるいは**butの手前は正しいけれど、後ろが間違っている**という選択肢がよくあります。そのような場合は**選択肢を切って、前後で判断すること**が有効になります。

7.は、最終段落the ability to **transcend local loyalties** and to approach world problems as a "citizen of the world"「**身の回りの世界への忠誠心を越えて**、『世界市民』として世界的な問題に取り組む能力」とあるだけで、**undesirable「望ましくない」**とは言っていないので、言い過ぎの選択肢として不適。

8.は、**第5段落第2文 With the rush to profitability in the global market「世界市場で利益追及に殺到する中」**に反するので不適。

構文図解

We are [in the midst of a crisis of massive proportions and grave
S V M massive proportionsとgrave global significanceの接続
global significance]. No, I do not mean the global economic crisis
M S V O
(that began in 2008). [At least] then everyone knew 〈that a crisis
関係代名詞のthat M M M S V 名詞節のthat
was at hand〉, and many world leaders worked quickly and
O S V M
desperately [to find solutions]. Indeed, consequences (for
不定詞 副詞的用法 M M S M
governments) were profound [if they did not find solutions], and
many governmentsの意味 V C governmentsを指す M
many were replaced [in consequence]. No, I mean a crisis (that goes
S V M M S V O 関係代名詞のthat M
largely unnoticed, like a cancer); a crisis that is likely to be, in the
前置詞のlike 関係代名詞のthat O′
long run, far more damaging to the future of democratic self-
比較級の強調「はるかに」
government: a worldwide crisis in education.

Radical changes are occurring [in what democratic societies teach
関係代名詞のwhat
S V 民主社会が若者に教える内容の根本的変化のこと M
the young], and these changes have not been well thought through.
S V think throughの受動態
[Thirsty for national profit], nations, and their systems of education,
Beingが省略された分詞構文 M S
are heedlessly discarding skills (that are needed to keep democracies
国益のために民主国家が機能するのに必要な技術が捨てられていること V O 関係代名詞のthat 不定詞 副詞的用法 M
alive). [If this trend continues], nations (all over the world) will soon
M S M V
be producing generations (of useful machines), [rather than complete
O M M
citizens who can think for themselves, criticize tradition, and
think for ～、criticize traditionとunderstandの3つの接続
understand the significance of another person's sufferings and
achievements]. The future (of the world's democracies) hangs [in the
S M V M
balance].

本文訳

私たちは、大規模かつ重大で世界的に重要で深刻な危機に瀕している最中だ。いや、私は2008年に始まった世界的な経済危機を意味しているのではない。少なくとも、その時にすべての人が危機は身近にあると知り、世界のリーダーの多くが、素早く必死になって解決策を探ろうと努めた。実際に、政府が解決策を見つけられないと、その影響は重大なもので、結果として多くの政権が入れ替わった。いや、私はガンのようにほとんど気付かれずに進行する危機のことを言っている。すなわち、長い目で見ると、民主的な自治の将来に、はるかに大きな害を与える可能性のある危機である、世界的な教育の危機だ。

民主社会が若者に教える内容の根本的な変化が起きており、こうした変化はよく考え抜かれてはいない。国益を渇望するあまり、国家、そしてその教育システムは、民主国家が機能し続けるのに必要な技術を、無配慮に捨てている。もしこの傾向が続くなら、世界中の国が、自分の頭で考えて、伝統を批判して、他人の苦しみや成果の意味を理解できる完全な市民よりも、役に立つ機械のような世代をやがて生み出していることになるだろう。世界の民主国家の将来は、不安定な状態にある。

語彙リスト

midst	名 真っただ中
massive	形 巨大な
proportion	名 規模
grave	形 重大な
significance	名 重要性
desperately	副 必死に
solution	名 解決策
consequence	名 影響
profound	形 重大な
cancer	名 ガン
in the long run	熟 長い目で見ると
self-government	名 自治
radical	形 根本的な
think through	熟 考え抜く
thirsty	形 渇望して
heedlessly	副 無配慮に
discard	動 捨てる
criticize	動 批判する
hang in the balance	熟 不安定な状態にある

▸単語10回CHECK 1 2 3 4 5 6 7 8 9 10

構文図解

What are these radical changes? The humanities and the arts are being cut away, [in both primary/secondary and college/university education, in virtually every nation of the world]. [Seen by policy-makers as useless frills], [at a time when nations must cut away all useless things in order to stay competitive in the global market], they are rapidly losing their place [in curricula], and also [in the minds and hearts of parents and children]. Indeed, 〈what we might call the humanistic aspects of science and social science〉 — the imaginative, creative aspect, and the aspect of rigorous critical thought — are losing ground [as nations prefer to pursue short-term profit by the cultivation of the useful and highly applied skills suited to profit-making].

（注記：these radical changes＝民主社会が若者に教える内容の根本的変化のこと／What＝C, are＝V, these radical changes＝S／The humanities and the arts＝S, are being cut away＝V, [in both … world]＝M／Seen＝分詞構文, [Seen … frills]＝M／as＝see A as Bのas／when＝関係副詞のwhen, [at a time … market]＝M／they＝the humanities and the artsを指す, S／are rapidly losing＝V, their place＝O, [in curricula]＝M, also＝M, [in the minds … children]＝M／Indeed＝M／what＝関係代名詞のwhat「いわゆる」, 〈what … science〉＝S／the imaginative, creative aspect, and the aspect of rigorous critical thought＝S′／are losing＝V, ground＝O／as＝理由のas, [as nations … profit-making]＝M／suited＝分詞の後置修飾）

This crisis is facing us, but we have not yet faced it. We go on [as if everything was business as usual], [when in reality great changes of emphasis are evident all over]. We haven't really thought hard [about these changes], we have not really chosen them, and yet they increasingly limit our future.

（注記：This crisis / it＝人文科学や芸術が切り捨てられている教育の危機／This crisis＝S, is facing＝V, us＝O, we＝S, have not yet faced＝V, it＝O／We＝S, go on＝V, [as if … usual]＝M, [when … all over]＝M／these changes＝科学や社会科学の人文学的側面が人気を失いつつあること／We＝S, haven't really thought＝V, hard＝M, [about these changes]＝M／we＝S, have not really chosen＝V, them＝O（these changesを指す）／they＝S（these changesを指す）, increasingly＝M, limit＝V, our future＝O）

[Given that economic growth is so eagerly sought by all nations, especially at this time of crisis], too few questions have been posed [about the direction of education, and, with it, of the world's democratic societies].

（注記：Given＝「～を考慮すると」, [Given … crisis]＝M／too few questions＝S, have been posed＝V, [about … societies]＝M／it＝educationを指す）

本文訳

これらの根本的な変化は何か？　世界のほぼすべての国で、初等・中等教育と大学教育の両方で、人文科学と芸術が切り捨てられている。国家が世界市場で競争力を保つために、すべての役に立たないものを切り捨てなければいけない時代に、政策立案者に役に立たない余分なものとみなされ、それらはカリキュラムや、親や子供の頭や心の中でも急速に居場所を失いつつある。実際に、国が利益を生み出すのに適した、有用で高度な応用技術を育成することによって、短期的な利益を追求することを好むので、自然科学と社会科学のいわゆる人文学的側面、すなわち想像的、独創的な側面や、厳密な批判的思考力の側面は、人気を失いつつある。

この危機は私たちの目の前にあるが、私たちはまだそれに立ち向かっていない。実際に、重要視されるものの重大な変化が明らかにいたるところで起きているのに、まるですべてが通常通りであるかのように、私たちはふるまう。私たちは、これらの変化についてそれほど一生懸命考えていなかったし、その変化を実際に選択したわけでもないが、その変化はますます私たちの未来を制限する。

特にこの危機的な時代に、すべての国家が経済成長をとても熱心に追及していることを考えると、教育やそれに伴う世界の民主社会の方向に関して、提起される疑問があまりに少なすぎる。

語彙リスト

the humanities	名	人文科学
cut away	熟	切り捨てる
virtually	副	ほぼ
policy-makers	名	政策立案者
frill	名	余分なもの
competitive	形	競争力のある
curricula	名	curriculum「カリキュラム」の複数形
humanistic	形	人文学の
aspect	名	側面
imaginative	形	想像力に富んだ
rigorous	形	厳密な
lose ground	熟	人気がなくなる
business as usual	熟	通常通りのこと
emphasis	名	重要視
evident	形	明白な
given that	熟	～を考慮すると

▸単語10回CHECK　1　2　3　4　5　6　7　8　9　10

構文図解

[With the rush to profitability in the global market], values 〈precious for the future of democracy, especially in an era of religious and economic anxiety〉, are [in danger of getting lost].

(With the rush to profitability in the global market: M / values: S / precious ～ anxiety: M, 形容詞の後置修飾 / are: V / in danger of getting lost: M)

The profit motive suggests [to many concerned leaders] 〈that science and technology are of crucial importance for the future health of their nations〉. We should have no objection 〈to good scientific and technical education〉, and I shall not suggest 〈that nations should stop trying to improve in this regard〉. My concern is 〈that other abilities, equally crucial, are at risk of getting lost in the competitive flurry, abilities crucial to the health of any democracy internally, and to the creation of a decent world culture capable of constructively addressing the world's most pressing problems〉.

(The profit motive: S / suggests: V / to many concerned leaders: M / that ～ nations: O, 名詞節のthat / We: S / should have: V / no objection: O / to good scientific and technical education: M / I: S / shall not suggest: V / that ～ regard: O, 名詞節のthat / this regard: 自然科学や科学技術の教育 / My concern: S / is: V / that ～ problems: C, 名詞節のthat / abilities, equally crucial: being省略の分詞構文 / abilities crucial: 形容詞の後置修飾 / flurry, abilities: 同格のカンマ「すなわち」 / and: to the health ～とto the creation ～の接続 / capable: 形容詞の後置修飾)

These abilities are associated with the humanities and the arts: the ability to think critically; the ability to transcend local loyalties and to approach world problems as a "citizen of the world"; and, finally, the ability to imagine sympathetically the predicaments of another person.

(These: 後方照応のthese / These abilities: S / are associated with: V / the humanities and the arts: O / to think: 不定詞 形容詞的用法（以下同じ） / and: to transcend ～とto approach の接続)

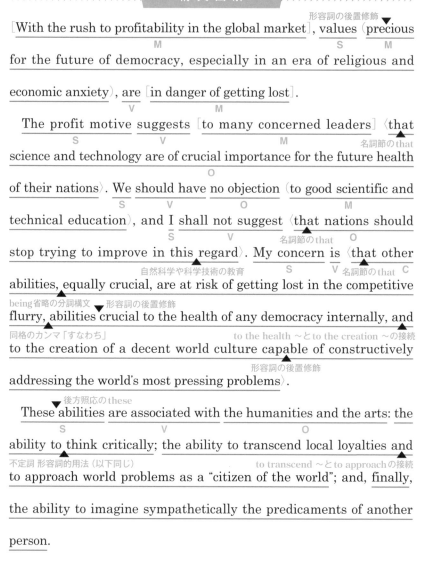

本文訳

世界市場で利益追及に殺到する中、民主主義の将来に貴重な価値観が、特に宗教と経済が不安の時代に失われる危機に瀕している。

この利益追求の動機が、多くの不安を抱くリーダーに対して、自然科学や科学技術が国家の健全な将来にとって不可欠の重要性を持つことを暗に示している。私たちは、優れた自然科学や科学技術の教育に対して異論はないはずだし、私は国家がこの点で改善しようとするのをやめるべきだという提案も決してしない。私の懸念は、同様に不可欠の他の能力、すなわちどんな民主国家でも、その内部の健全さにとって不可欠の能力、そして世界の最も急を要する問題に、建設的に取り組むことのできるまともな世界文化の創造に不可欠な能力が、競争の混乱の中で損なわれる危機に瀕していることだ。

次に述べる能力は、人文科学と芸術に関連している。すなわち、批判的思考力、身の周りの世界への忠誠心を越えて、「世界市民」として世界的な問題に取り組む能力、そして最後は、他人の苦境を共感して想像する能力のことだ。

語彙リスト

□	rush	名 殺到
□	profitability	名 利益性
□	era	名 時代
□	crucial	形 不可欠な
□	regard	名 点
□	flurry	名 混乱
□	decent	形 まともな
□	address	動 ～に取り組む
□	critically	副 批判的に
□	transcend	動 越える
□	loyalty	名 忠誠心
□	approach	動 ～に取り組む
□	sympathetically	副 共感して
□	predicament	名 苦境

▸単語10回CHECK 1 2 3 4 5 6 7 8 9 10

We are in the midst of a crisis of massive proportions and grave global significance. No, I do not mean the global economic crisis that began in 2008. At least then everyone knew that a crisis was at hand, and many world leaders worked quickly and desperately to find solutions. Indeed, consequences for governments were profound if they did not find solutions, and many were replaced in consequence. No, I mean a crisis that goes largely unnoticed, like a cancer; a crisis that is likely to be, in the long run, far more damaging to the future of democratic self-government: a worldwide crisis in education.

Radical changes are occurring in what democratic societies teach the young, and these changes have not been well thought through. Thirsty for national profit, nations, and their systems of education, are heedlessly discarding skills that are needed to keep democracies alive. If this trend continues, nations all over the world will soon be producing generations of useful machines, rather than complete citizens who can think for themselves, criticize tradition, and understand the significance of another person's sufferings and achievements. The future of the world's democracies hangs in the balance.

What are these radical changes? The humanities and the arts are being cut away, in both primary/secondary and college/university education, in virtually every nation of the world. Seen by policy-makers as useless frills, at a time when nations must cut away all useless things in order to stay competitive in the global market, they are rapidly losing their place in curricula, and also in the minds and hearts of parents and children. Indeed, what we might call the humanistic aspects of science and social science — the imaginative, creative aspect, and the aspect of rigorous critical thought — are losing ground as nations prefer to pursue short-term profit by the cultivation of the useful and highly applied skills suited to profit-making.

This crisis is facing us, but we have not yet faced it. We go on as if everything were business as usual, when in reality great changes of emphasis are evident all over. We haven't really thought hard about these changes, we have not really chosen them, and yet they increasingly limit our future.

Given that economic growth is so eagerly sought by all nations, especially at this time of crisis, too few questions have been posed about the direction of education, and, with it, of the world's democratic societies. With the rush to profitability in the global market, values precious for the future of democracy, especially in an era of religious and economic anxiety, are in danger of getting lost.

The profit motive suggests to many concerned leaders that science and technology are of crucial importance for the future health of their nations. We should have no objection to good scientific and technical education, and I shall not suggest that nations should stop trying to improve in this regard. My concern is that other abilities, equally crucial, are at risk of getting lost in the competitive flurry, abilities crucial to the health of any democracy internally, and to the creation of a decent world culture capable of constructively addressing the world's most pressing problems.

These abilities are associated with the humanities and the arts: the ability to think critically; the ability to transcend local loyalties and to approach world problems as a "citizen of the world"; and, finally, the ability to imagine sympathetically the predicaments of another person.

▶音読10回CHECK 1 2 3 4 5 6 7 8 9 10

背景知識が
広がるコラム

BACKGROUND KNOWLEDGE

人文科学と自然科学

本問で登場した**the humanities**「**人文科学**」と**science**「**自然科学**」について、理解を深めていきます。**自然科学**は**natural science**と言うこともあります。

高校までは文系・理系というように学問を分類してきましたが、大学に入ると、**人文科学・自然科学と学問を分類**します。**人文科学**とは、**人間や人間が作り出したものを研究の対象とする学問**で、**自然科学**とは、**自然を対象として、その法則を見出す学問**です。これに、**社会をもう1つの対象**としてみると、**social science**「**社会科学**」という分野も存在します。

人文科学には、**哲学・倫理学・美学・歴史学・考古学・言語学・文学・芸術学・教育学・心理学**などがあります。一方、**自然科学**には、**物理学・化学・生物学・天文学や数学・医学・農学・工学**などがあります。**高校までの理科**をイメージすると、自然科学と重なる分野があります。ちなみに、**社会科学**は、**人間を構成員とした社会の様々な面を科学的に探求する学術分野**です。例えば、**経済学・法学・政治学・社会学**などがあります。

本文にあったように、欧米の大学では、**自然科学が就職や職業に直結するために人気が出て、人文科学が就職や職業に結び付かないケースがあるために軽視され、志願者数の減少と共に、学部も減少している**ようです。本文のように、**人文科学はすべての職業に通じる大切な真理を学べる学問である**ことを忘れてはいけないのでしょう。

問題 8

生物

生物学的複雑性

別冊p.34／制限時間20分／519 words

解答

1 a　2 b　3 d　4 d　5 b

解説

1

タンポポと虫は

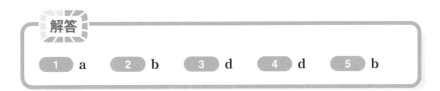

(a) 人間や宇宙空間からやってくる宇宙人とさえ、同じように複雑だ。

(b) 既知の宇宙全体で見つけることができる。

(c) 複雑なように見えるかもしれないが、実際は岩や雲のように、それらはとても単純だ。

(d) 他の複雑な生き物とは別に、議論して説明する必要がある。

第1段落最終文Chimps ～ **people and worms and dandelions** and bacteria and **galactic aliens** are **the stuff of biology**.「チンパンジー、～、**人間**、**虫**、**タンポポ**、バクテリア、**銀河の宇宙人は生物学の世界のものだ**」と、第2段落第2文**Biology** is the study of **complicated things** ～.「**生物学は**、～な**複雑なもの**の研究だ」から、**(a) are complicated in the same way as humans or even aliens from outer space are.** が正解。

不正解の選択肢を見ていくと、(c)は、上記の2つの文より、単純ではないので不適。(b), (d)は本文に記述なし。

2

車やコンピューターのような複雑なものは、～と著者は信じている。

(a) 特定の目的のために設計されたものだから面白くない。

(b) 生きているものでなくても、生物学の一部として議論されるかもしれない。

（c） 実際は、物理学の研究の一分野だ。
（d） 生物学の研究とは異なるものとみなすべきだ。

cars or computersをスキャンすると、**第2段落第4文man-made artefacts like computers and cars** will seem to provide exceptions. から、人工物の具体例として挙げられていることがわかる。後続の**同段落第5文後半they are not alive, 同段落最終文 ～ they should be firmly treated as biological objects.**「**それらは生物学的物体としてしっかりと扱われるべきだ**」から、**(b) may be discussed as being a part of biology even though they are not alive.**が正解とわかる。

不正解の選択肢を見ていくと、(a)は、**第2段落第5文They are complicated and obviously designed for a purpose**, ～. から、**because以下は正しい記述**だが、それより前の**are not of interest**「**面白くない**」**との記述はない**ので不適。解法 POINT ❹ で扱ったように、**選択肢を切って考える**とよい。(c), (d)は、第2段落最終文に反するので不適。

3

動物の研究を専門にする科学者は
（a） 人間は、魚よりもロブスターと密接な関係にあると信じている。
（b） ロブスターはある種の昆虫と分類されるべきだという一致した見解に達している。
（c） 現在、昆虫を決して動物と見なしてはいけないと理解している。
（d） ロブスターが魚として説明されることを受け入れないだろう。

(d)は、**第3段落第5文Zoologists can become quite upset about this**「**動物学者は、このこと（ほとんどの料理本で、ロブスターを魚と分類していること）で大いに悩む可能性がある**」と一致するので、正解。

不正解の選択肢を見ていくと、(a)は、**第3段落第5文後半部分since fish are far closer kin to humans than they are to lobsters**「**魚はロブスターより人間にはるかに近い親類なので**」に反する。(a)は、**人間がロブスターと近い**だが、本文では**魚が人間に近い**とあり、記述が異なる点に注意する。

(b)は**同段落第7文Zoologically speaking, lobsters are certainly not insects.「動物学的に言うと、ロブスターは、間違いなく昆虫ではない**」に反するので不適。(c)は**同段落第8文**They are animals, but then **so are insects** and so are we.「それらは動物だが、**それなら昆虫もそうだ（動物だ）**し、私たちもそうだ」に反するので不適。

4

著者によると、
(a)　言語と語彙は両方とも明らかに生物学の対象だ。
(b)　法律家とコックは、言葉を注意深く使わない専門家の例だ。
(c)　どんな言葉の意味も神聖なので、変えるべきではない。
(d)　言葉は、私たちが当面の目的を最適の形でかなえるのに変えられる道具だ。

第3段落第3文 For different purposes we find it convenient to use words in different senses.「異なる目的のために、私たちは、異なる意味で言葉を使うことを都合がよいと思う」は、要するに**目的によって、同じ言葉を違う意味で使うことがある**ということで、(d)の**words are tools we can adapt to best suit our immediate purpose**と一致するので、正解。

(c)は同文に反する。(b)は、**第3段落第4文、第5文**及び第10文から判断する。簡単にまとめると、まず、**ロブスターという言葉も、コックが使うか動物学者が使うかで意味合いが異なる**とあり、次に法律家もコックも独自の言葉の使い方をするとある。どちらにも、法律家とコックが言葉を注意深く使わない例として挙がっているわけではないので不適。

5

機械が生命の存在を知らせるものと言われている理由は、
(a)　いくつかの複雑な機械が、他の惑星で発見されたからだ。
(b)　何らかの生命体が、機械の複雑な設計に着手するのに必要だろうからだ。
(c)　これらの複雑な機械的物体が、将来生物学上の生命に取って代わると予言されているからだ。
(d)　それらは、化石や骸骨（がいこつ）、死体のない場所で見つかることがよくあるからだ。

第3段落第13文 Machines are the direct products of living objects; they derive their complexity and design from living objects, and they are diagnostic of the existence of life on a planet.「**機械は生き物の直接的な産物だ。それらは、その複雑さや設計を、生き物に由来しており、それらは、ある惑星の生命の存在の判断材料になる**」は、要するに**機械の複雑さや設計は、何らかの生命体をヒントにして生まれている**ということなので、**(b) some form of life would be necessary to initiate the complex design of a machine.** が正解。それ以外の選択肢は本文に記述なし。

構文図解

We animals are the most complicated things [in the known
S V C M
universe]. The universe (that we know), [of course], is a tiny
S 関係代名詞のthat M M 比較級の強調「いっそう」 V C
fragment (of the actual universe). There may be yet more
M M V more complicated objectsを指す
complicated objects [than us] [on other planets], and some (of them)
S M M S M
may already know [about us]. But this doesn't alter the point (that I
V M 前文の内容を指す S V O 関係代名詞のthat M
want to make). Complicated things, everywhere, deserve (a very
S M V M
special kind of) explanation. We want 〈to know how they came into
how ~ existenceとwhy ~ complicatedの接続 O S V 不定詞 名詞的用法 O complicated thingsを指す
existence and why they are so complicated〉. The explanation, [as I
complicated thingsを指す S 関係代名詞のas M
shall argue], is likely to be broadly the same [for complicated things
V M C M
everywhere in the universe]; the same [for us, for chimpanzees,
The explanation ~ broadlyの省略 M'
worms, oak trees and monsters from outer space]. [On the other
The explanationを指す M
hand], it will not be the same [for what I shall call 'simple' things,
S V C「いわゆる」 M rocks ~ quarksを指す
such as rocks, clouds, rivers, galaxies and quarks]. These are the
S V C
stuff (of physics). Chimps and dogs and bats and cockroaches and
M S
people and worms and dandelions and bacteria and galactic aliens
are the stuff (of biology).
V C M

The difference is one (of complexity of design). Biology is the study
S V C M S V C
(of complicated things that give the appearance of having been
関係代名詞のthat M
designed for a purpose).

本文訳

私たち動物は、既知の宇宙の中で最も複雑なものだ。もちろん、私たちが知っている宇宙は、実際の宇宙のごく小さな断片に過ぎない。他の惑星には、私たちよりいっそう複雑な物体があるかもしれず、そのいくつかは、私たちのことをすでに知っているかもしれない。しかし、そのことによって、私の言いたいことが変わるわけではない。複雑なものは、どこであっても非常に特別な説明に値する。私たちは、どうやってそれらが誕生して、なぜそれらがそんなに複雑なのかを知りたいと思っている。私が主張していくように、その説明は、宇宙のいたるところにいる複雑なものに対しては、およそ同じである可能性が高い。すなわち、私たちに対しても、チンパンジー、虫、*オークの木、そして宇宙から来た怪物に対しても同じ可能性が高いということだ。それに対して、その説明は、岩、雲、川、銀河、そして*クオークのようないわゆる「単純な」ものに対しては同じではないだろう。これらは物理学の世界のものだ。チンパンジー、犬、コウモリ、コオロギ、人間、虫、タンポポ、バクテリア、銀河の宇宙人は生物学の世界のものだ。

違いは、設計の複雑さにある。生物学は、ある目的のために設計されたかのように見える複雑なものに対する研究だ。

*「オークの木」は、家具などに使うカシなどの木のこと。

*「クオーク」は、物資を構成する最も基本的な粒子。

語彙リスト

□	complicated	形 複雑な
□	known	形 既知の
□	tiny	形 微小な
□	fragment	名 断片
□	yet	副 いっそう
□	deserve	動 ～に値する
□	come into existence	熟 誕生する
□	worm	名 （足のない）虫
□	oak tree	名 オークの木
□	galaxy	名 銀河
□	quark	名 クオーク（素粒子の構成要素）
□	stuff	名 もの
□	physics	名 物理学
□	cockroach	名 コオロギ
□	dandelion	名 タンポポ
□	give the appearance of	熟 ～のように見える

▸単語10回CHECK 1 □ 2 □ 3 □ 4 □ 5 □ 6 □ 7 □ 8 □ 9 □ 10 □

構文図解

Physics is the study (of simple things that do not tempt us to invoke
S V C 関係代名詞のthat M 前置詞のlike
design). [At first sight], man-made artefacts (like computers and
M S man-made artefactsを指す M
cars) will seem to provide exceptions. They are complicated and
V O S V C man-made artefactsを指す
obviously designed [for a purpose], yet they are not alive, and they
C M S V C S
are made of metal and plastic [rather than of flesh and blood]. [In
V man-made artefactsを指す O M M
my view] they should be firmly treated [as biological objects].
S V 人間が作った人工物が生物学的物体として扱われるべきだということ M

The reader's reaction (to this) may be ⟨to ask, 'Yes, but are they
S M V 不定詞 名詞的用法 C man-made artefactsを指す
really biological objects?⟩' Words are our servants, not our masters.
S V C B, not A「AではなくてB」 C′
形式目的語のit
[For different purposes] we find it convenient ⟨to use words in
M S V O C 不定詞 名詞的用法 O′
different senses⟩. Most cookery books class lobsters as fish. Zoologists
料理本でロブスターを魚に分類していること S V A as B S
can become quite upset [about this], [pointing out that lobsters could
V C M 分詞構文 名詞節のthat
with greater justice call humans fish], [since fish are far closer kin to
M 理由のsince M 比較級の強調「はるかに」
humans than they are to lobsters]. And, [talking of justice and
fishを指す kinの省略 分詞構文 M
lobsters], I understand ⟨that a court of law recently had to decide
S V 名詞節のthat O
whether lobsters were insects or 'animals' (it bore upon whether
名詞節のwhether「～かどうか」 whether lobsters ～ 'animals' を指す 名詞節のwhether「～かどうか」
people should be allowed to boil them alive)⟩. [Zoologically
lobstersを指す M
speaking], lobsters are certainly not insects. They are animals, but
S V C S V C
then so are insects and so are we.
M M V S M V S

本文訳

物理学は、私たちに設計を思い起こさせることのない単純なものの研究だ。一見すると、コンピューターや車のような人工物は、例外であるかのように思えるだろう。それらは複雑で、明らかにある目的のために設計されているが、生きてはおらず、肉や血液ではなくて金属やプラスチックでできている。私の考えでは、それらは生物学的物体として、しっかりと扱われるべきだ。

読者はこれに対する反応として、「そうですね、でもそれらは本当に生物学的物体ですか？」と尋ねるかもしれない。言葉は私たちの召使であって、主人ではない。異なる目的のために、私たちは、異なる意味で言葉を使うことを都合がよいと思う。ほとんどの料理本は、ロブスターを魚と分類する。動物学者は、魚はロブスターより人間にはるかに近い親類なので、ロブスターが人間を魚と呼ぶほうがよほど正当だと指摘して、このことで大いに悩む可能性がある。そして、正当性とロブスターと言えば、私は、裁判所が最近、ロブスターは昆虫か「動物」か（人がそれらを生きたままゆでることが許されるべきかどうかということに影響していた）の判決を下さなければならなかったことを知っている。動物学的に言うと、ロブスターは、間違いなく昆虫ではない。それらは動物だが、それなら昆虫もそうだし、私たちもそうだ。

語彙リスト

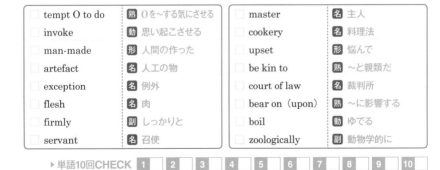

tempt O to do	熟	Oを～する気にさせる
invoke	動	思い起こさせる
man-made	形	人間の作った
artefact	名	人工の物
exception	名	例外
flesh	名	肉
firmly	副	しっかりと
servant	名	召使
master	名	主人
cookery	名	料理法
upset	形	悩んで
be kin to	熟	～と親類だ
court of law	名	裁判所
bear on（upon）	熟	～に影響する
boil	動	ゆでる
zoologically	副	動物学的に

▸単語10回CHECK 1 2 3 4 5 6 7 8 9 10

構文図解

There is little point [in getting worked up about the way different people use words (although in my nonprofessional life I am quite prepared to get worked up about people who boil lobsters alive)].

M V S M

the way SV「SがVする方法」

Cooks and lawyers need to use words [in their own special ways].

S V O M

Never mind 〈whether cars and computers are 'really' biological objects〉. The point is 〈that if anything of that degree of complexity were found on a planet, we should have no hesitation in concluding that life existed, or had once existed, on that planet〉. Machines are the direct products (of living objects); they derive their complexity and design from living objects, and they are diagnostic [of the existence of life on a planet]. The same goes [for fossils, skeletons and dead bodies].

M V O（名詞節のwhether「～かどうか」）

S V C（名詞節のthat）

名詞節のthat

S V C M（they: machinesを指す）

S V A（from B）

S V C M（they: machinesを指す）

S V M

本文訳

（自分の仕事を離れれば、ロブスターを生きたままゆでる人のことで大いに感情的にもなるだろうが）、様々な人が言葉を使う方法について感情的になるのはほとんど意味がない。コックと法律家は、自分独自のやり方で言葉を使う必要がある。車やコンピューターが「本当に」生物学的物体かどうかは、気にしなくていい。重要なのは、もしある惑星で、その程度の複雑さのものが見つかったなら、私たちは、その惑星に生命が存在している、あるいはかつて存在していたとためらわずに結論を下すべきだ。機械は生き物の直接的な産物だ。それらは、その複雑さや設計を生き物に由来しており、それらは、ある惑星における生命の存在の判断材料になる。同じことが化石、骸骨（がいこつ）、死体にも当てはまる。

語彙リスト

There is little point in doing.	熟	～してもほとんど意味がない。
get worked up	熟	感情的になる
degree	名	程度
complexity	名	複雑さ
hesitation	名	ためらい
conclude	動	結論を下す
derive A from B	熟	BからAを得る
diagnostic of ～	熟	～の判断に役立つ
fossil	名	化石
skeleton	名	骸骨

▸単語10回CHECK 1 2 3 4 5 6 7 8 9 10

We animals are the most complicated things in the known universe. The universe that we know, of course, is a tiny fragment of the actual universe. There may be yet more complicated objects than us on other planets, and some of them may already know about us. But this doesn't alter the point that I want to make. Complicated things, everywhere, deserve a very special kind of explanation. We want to know how they came into existence and why they are so complicated. The explanation, as I shall argue, is likely to be broadly the same for complicated things everywhere in the universe; the same for us, for chimpanzees, worms, oak trees and monsters from outer space. On the other hand, it will not be the same for what I shall call 'simple' things, such as rocks, clouds, rivers, galaxies and quarks. These are the stuff of physics. Chimps and dogs and bats and cockroaches and people and worms and dandelions and bacteria and galactic aliens are the stuff of biology.

The difference is one of complexity of design. Biology is the study of complicated things that give the appearance of having been designed for a purpose. Physics is the study of simple things that do not tempt us to invoke design. At first sight, man-made artefacts like computers and cars will seem to provide exceptions. They are complicated and obviously designed for a purpose, yet they are not alive, and they are made of metal and plastic rather than of flesh and blood. In my view they should be firmly treated as biological objects.

The reader's reaction to this may be to ask, 'Yes, but are they really biological objects?' Words are our servants, not our masters. For different purposes we find it convenient to use words in different senses. Most cookery books class lobsters as fish. Zoologists can become quite upset about this, pointing out that lobsters could with greater justice call humans fish, since fish are far closer kin to humans than they are to lobsters. And, talking of justice and lobsters, I understand that a court of law recently had to decide whether lobsters were insects or 'animals' (it bore upon whether people should be allowed to boil them alive). Zoologically speaking, lobsters are certainly not insects. They are animals, but then so are insects and so are we. There is little point in getting worked up about the way different people use words (although in my nonprofessional life I am quite prepared to get worked up about people who boil lobsters alive). Cooks and lawyers need to use words in their own special ways. Never mind whether cars and computers are 'really' biological objects. The point is that if anything of that degree of complexity were found on a planet, we should have no hesitation in concluding that life existed, or had once existed, on that planet. Machines are the direct products of living objects; they derive their complexity and design from living objects, and they are diagnostic of the existence of life on a planet. The same goes for fossils, skeletons and dead bodies.

▸音読10回CHECK 1 2 3 4 5 6 7 8 9 10

背景知識が広がるコラム

BACKGROUND KNOWLEDGE

生きたロブスターの煮沸（しゃふつ）を禁止する法律

本文で、**料理本ではロブスターを魚と分類するが、動物学者はロブスターを魚とはみなさない**という記述がありました。**裁判所がロブスターは昆虫か動物かの判断を下さなければならなかった**という記述がありましたが、実際にスイスで**ロブスターに関する裁判**がありました。

この裁判は、鳥類や哺乳類は保護してきたのに、**エビやカニは無視している状況を疑問視し、生きたまま煮沸するのは非人道的だ**という主張から始まったものです。

この裁判によって、**ロブスターを含めた甲殻類は、痛みを感じる可能性がある高度な神経系を保持している**という研究結果を踏まえて、**まだ生きている場合、調理のために熱湯に入れることを禁止する新たな法律**が成立しました。

以後は、調理前に気絶させるか、即座に絶命させることが必要になりました。また、輸送する際にも、ロブスターを含む甲殻類を氷詰めの状態にして運ぶことを禁止して、自然の状態で保管しなければならないとしました。

ちなみに、**ロブスターは魚類ではなく甲殻類**ですが、その他にも**区別が難しい動物**がいます。例えば、コウモリは鳥類に分類されると思いますか？　答えは、ノーです。**コウモリは哺乳類に分類**されます。**コウモリには羽毛がなく、子どもを母乳で育てるので哺乳類**とされます。一方で、**ペンギンは哺乳類に分類**されると思いますか？　これまた、答えはノーです。**ペンギンは殻のある卵を産み、羽毛で覆われているので鳥類**に分類されます。

飛行能力のあるコウモリは哺乳類で、飛行能力のないペンギンは鳥類であることからも、**「飛ぶかどうか」だけでは、鳥類とは判断できず、子どもの産み方（卵で産むか否か）、皮膚の様子（羽毛で覆われているか否か）**などで判断されるとわかります。

問題 9

文化

芸術の儀式からの解放

別冊 p.38 ／制限時間 25 分／ 555 words

解答

(1) ④　(2) ②　(3) ③　(4) ①　(5) ①

解説

(1)

次の考えのうち、段落 [A] で見つからないものはどれか。

① 伝統は布に例えることができる。

② 魔法と宗教は異なる歴史上の時期に属する。

③ 芸術作品は、古代の儀式の一部だった。

④ 芸術作品は、美しいものと恐ろしいものを混在させたものでなければならない。

NOT 問題なので消去法で対処する。①は**段落 [A] 第 1 文** The uniqueness of a work of art is inseparable from its being part of **the fabric of tradition**.「芸術作品の独自性は、それが**伝統という織物**の一部であることから切り離せない」から、段落 [A] にあると判断して、不適。**fabric は「織物」、すなわち「布地」で cloth より堅い単語。**

②は**段落 [A] 第 5 文** We know that the earliest art works originated in the service of a ritual — **first the magical, then the religious kind.**「私たちは、最も初期の芸術作品が、**最初は魔術的な儀式、それから宗教的な類の儀式に奉仕すること**から始まったと知っている」から、**魔法と宗教は異なる時期に属すると推論できる**ので、段落 [A] にあると判断して、不適。

③は**段落 [A] 第 6 文** It is significant that the existence of **the work of art** with reference to its aura **was never entirely separated from its ritual function.**「そのオーラに関連する**芸術作品の存在は、その儀式的機能からは決して完全には切り離せない**という

ことが重要だ」から、③も段落[A]にあると判断して、不適。

④は、**段落[A]第3文**で、**古代のビーナス像を、ギリシャ人は崇拝の対象とみなし、中世の聖職者は恐ろしい偶像とみなした**とあるだけで、**「美と恐怖が混在」という記述はない**ので、**段落[A]からは読み取れない**と判断して正解となる。

(2)

次の考えのうち、段落[B]で見つけられるものはどれか。

① 芸術の儀式的要素は、常に不変のままだ。
② 芸術の儀式的要素は、芸術作品が宗教的でないときでさえ見出すことができる。
③ 芸術の儀式的要素は、写真が発明されるまで、不変のままだった。
④ 多くの社会主義的考えは、写真技術に例えることができる。

段落[B]第1文This ritualistic basis, however remote, **is still recognizable even in the most irreligious forms of the cult of beauty.**「**この儀式的な基盤は**、どんなに昔のものであろうと、**美を礼賛する最も無宗教な形式の中にさえ依然として見出すことができる**」から、②が正解。**This ritualistic basis**とは、前文の「本物の**芸術作品**の独自の価値は、**儀式的なものがその基盤にある**」ことを指す。**the cult of beauty**「**美の礼賛**」は、**芸術作品についての表現**なので、**本文のthe most irreligious forms of the cult of beauty**は、**②のthe art work is not religiousと同義**となる。

不正解の選択肢を見ていくと、①は**段落[B]第2文** However this secular cult of beauty, developed during the Renaissance and prevailing for three centuries, clearly showed **how art's ritualistic basis was declining**.「しかし、この非宗教的な美の礼賛は、ルネッサンス期に現れて3世紀の間普及したが、**芸術の儀式的基盤がどのように衰退していくか**をはっきりと示すものだった」から、**いつも不変ではないとわかる**ので、不適。

③も、**同段落第3文**から、**この後に写真が発明されたとわかるので、写真の発明以前に芸術の儀式的要素が変化している(=衰退している)とわかる**ので、不適。

④は、**段落［B］第３文**に、**社会主義の台頭と同時に、写真が発見された**とあるだけで、「**社会主義的考えを写真技術に例える**」**という記述はない**ので、不適。

(3)

段落［B］で、『「純粋な」芸術という考えは、芸術の社会的機能だけではなく、主題によるいかなる分類をも否定した』という一節がある。次のうち、その一節の意味を最もよく言い表しているのはどれか。

① 具体的なものに関する場合に限るが、芸術が社会に何らかの形で役に立つという考え。

② 芸術家がそうだと考える場合に限るが、芸術が社会に何らかの形で役に立つという考え。

③ 芸術は社会に何の役にも立たないし、特定の何かでなくてもよいという考え。

④ いかなる分類においても、芸術だけが社会に役に立つという考え。

段落［B］の最終文**denied any social function of art**は、**"pure" art**という表現からも、**芸術が何らかの社会的役割を果たすことを否定している**ことを意味するので、③の**of no use to society**と同義とわかる。①、②はof some use of societyとあるので、不適。一方で、**denied ~ any categorizing by subject matter**「**主題によるいかなる分類をも否定した**」は、③の**does not have to be about anything in particular**「**特定の何かでなくてもよい**」と同義なので、③が正解。

④は、**芸術だけが実際に社会に役に立つという排他的な表現はない**ので、不適。

(4)

次のうち、段落［C］の内容を最もよく要約しているものはどれか。

① 一度芸術が機械的に複製されると、その役割は完全に変わった。

② 一度写真が発明されると、芸術作品の必要性はなくなった。

③ 写真は、政治の儀式を完全に変えた。

④ 芸術は、マイナスの方法でのみ、儀式から解放された。

段落 [C] 第1文 An analysis of art in the age of mechanical reproduction leads us to an all-important insight「機械的な複製時代の芸術を分析することで、私たちはある非常に重要な洞察に至る」とあり、コロンの後ろで、**an all-important insight が具体化**されている。

論理 POINT ④ a ＋ 抽象名詞 は抽象の目印

a ＋ 抽象名詞 は、抽象表現の一種なので、後ろから具体説明が続きます。an idea ／ a discovery ／ an insight などを見たら、それぞれ「**ある考え**」、「**ある発見**」、「**ある洞察**」と訳し、**次の文からそれらが具体化されると推測**して「**すなわち**」と補って、見えない文のつながりを見抜きましょう。

本文では、**for the first time in world history, mechanical reproduction frees the work of art from its dependence on ritual.「世界史上初めて、機械的な複製が、芸術作品をその儀式への依存から解放する」**が、**an all-important insight の具体的説明**となる。

続いて、**段落 [C] 最終文** Instead of being based on ritual, it begins to be based on another practice: **politics**.「儀式に基づく代わりに、それ（芸術）はもう1つの慣習、すなわち**政治**に基づき始める」から、**芸術が儀式から解放されて政治と結びつく**とわかるので、① **Once art was mechanically reproduced, its role was completely changed.** が正解とわかる。

上記の理解から、③のような**政治の儀式を変えたという記述はない**ので、不適。④は but までは正しいが、「**マイナスの方法で**」**という記述はない**ので不適。②は、**段落 [C] 第2文**には、「**写真が発明されてから、『本物』を求めることは意味がなくなった**」とあるだけで、**芸術作品の必要性がなくなったとは書かれていない**ので不適。

(5)

次のうち、段落 [D] で説明されている洞窟にある動物の絵画の役割を最もよく表しているものはどれか。

① それらは、人間が見ることができたが、主に超自然的なものだった。

② それらは、主に人間に見られるためのものだったが、超自然的な機能も備えていた。

③ それらは、魔術のための道具を使う時だけ、人間が見ることができた。

④ それらは、魔術のための道具を使う精霊が見ることができた。

①が、**段落［D］第6文**He did **expose it to his fellow men**, but **in the main it was meant for the spirits**.「彼は、それ（洞窟の壁画に描かれた鹿）を**仲間たちに実際に見せた**が、**主に、それは霊魂のためのもの**だった」と一致するので正解。本文の**expose it to his fellow men**が選択肢の**they could be viewed by humans**に**パラフレーズ**されて、本文の**in the main it was meant for the spirits**は選択肢の**Their function was mainly supernatural**に**パラフレーズ**されている。

不正解の選択肢を見ていくと、同文の「**主に霊魂のためのものだった**」から、②の「**それら（洞窟の動物の壁画）は主に人間に見られるためのものだった**」**がおかしいとわかる**ので、不適。

③はbutまでは正しいが、but以下がおかしい。**段落［D］第5文**The deer portrayed by ~ was an **instrument of magic**.「~が描いた鹿は**魔術のための道具**だった」とあるが、**魔術のための道具を使うときだけ人間が洞窟の絵画を見ることができるとは書かれていない**ので不適。

④も本文に記述なし。

構文図解

a work of artを指す

[A] The uniqueness (of a work of art) is inseparable [from its being
S M V C 動名詞の主語と動名詞

part of the fabric of tradition]. This tradition itself is thoroughly alive
M S V C

and extremely changeable. An ancient statue (of Venus), [for
C S M M

example], stood [in a different traditional context with the Greeks,
V different ~ than... M

who made it an object of worship], [than with the priests of the
an ancient statue of Venusを指す differentと対応している

Middle Ages, who viewed it as a frightening idol]. They both,
the Greeksとthe priests of the Middle Agesを指す S

however, had to face up to its uniqueness, that is, its aura. We know
M V O O′ S V

⟨that the earliest art works originated in the service of a ritual —
名詞節のthat O 形式主語のit

first the magical, then the religious kind⟩. It is significant ⟨that the
S V C 名詞節のthat S′

existence of the work of art with reference to its aura was never

entirely separated from its ritual function⟩. [In other words], the
M S

unique value (of the "authentic" work of art) has its basis [in ritual].
M it (=this ritualistic basis) isの省略 V O M

[B] This ritualistic basis, [however remote], is still recognizable
「本物の」芸術作品の独自の価値は、儀式がその基盤にあること M V C

[even in the most irreligious forms of the cult of beauty]. However
M M

this secular cult (of beauty), [developed during the Renaissance and
S M 分詞構文 M

prevailing for three centuries], clearly showed ⟨how art's ritualistic
M V 疑問副詞「どのように〜か」 O

basis was declining⟩.

本文訳

[A] 芸術作品の独自性は、それが伝統という織物の一部であることから切り離せない。この伝統そのものが、完全に生きており、非常に変わりやすい。例えば、古代のビーナス像は、それを崇拝の対象としたギリシャ人のいる状況と、それを恐ろしい偶像とみなす中世の聖職者のいる状況という異なる伝統的な状況の中に存在していた。しかし、彼らは両方とも、その独自性、すなわちその像が放つオーラに直面しなければならなかった。私たちは、最も初期の芸術作品が、最初は魔術的な儀式、それから宗教的な類の儀式に奉仕することから始まったと知っている。そのオーラに関連する芸術作品の存在は、その儀式的機能からは決して完全には切り離せないということが重要だ。すなわち、「本物の」芸術作品の独自の価値は、儀式がその基盤にある。
[B] この儀式的な基盤は、どんなに昔のものであろうと、美を礼賛する最も無宗教な形式の中にさえ、依然として見出すことができる。しかし、この非宗教的な美の礼賛は、ルネッサンス期に現れて3世紀の間普及したが、芸術の儀式的な基盤がどのように衰退していくかをはっきりと示した。

語彙リスト

work of art	名 芸術作品
inseparable	形 分けられない
fabric	名 織物
thoroughly	副 完全に
statue	名 像
context	名 状況
worship	名 崇拝
priest	名 聖職者
view A as B	熟 AをBとみなす
frightening	形 恐ろしい
idol	名 偶像
face up to	熟 ～を直視する
aura	名 雰囲気、オーラ
originate in	熟 ～から起こる
ritual	名 儀式
religious	形 宗教的な
significant	形 重大な
with reference to	熟 ～に関して
authentic	形 本物の
cult	名 礼賛
secular	形 非宗教的な
prevail	動 普及する

▸単語10回CHECK 1 2 3 4 5 6 7 8 9 10

構文図解

[With the discovery of the first truly revolutionary means of reproduction, photography, simultaneously with the rise of socialism], art sensed the approaching crisis (which has become evident a century later). [At the time], art reacted [with the doctrine of "art for art's sake]." This gave rise to the idea (of "pure" art), [which not only denied any social function of art but also any categorizing by subject matter].

芸術が「芸術のための芸術」という主義で反応したこと

not only A but also B

[C] An analysis (of art) (in the age of mechanical reproduction) leads us [to an all-important insight]: [for the first time in world history], mechanical reproduction frees the work (of art) [from its dependence on ritual]. [From a photographic negative], [for example], one can make (any number of) prints; 〈to ask for the "authentic" print〉 makes no sense. But [the instant the standard of authenticity ceases to be applicable to artistic production], the total function (of art) is reversed. [Instead of being based on ritual], it begins 〈to be based on another practice: politics〉.

一般人を指す

不定詞 名詞的用法

the instant S' V'「S'がV'するとすぐに」

artを指す

不定詞 名詞的用法

[D] Works (of art) are received and valued [on different levels]. Two opposite types stand out; [with one], the accent is [on the cult value]; [with the other], [on the exhibition value of the work].

本文訳

社会主義の台頭と同時に、写真という最初の真に革命的な複製手段が発見されたことにより、芸術は、1世紀後に明白になる危機が近づいているのを感じていた。その当時、芸術は、「芸術のための芸術」という主義で反応した。このことは、「純粋な」芸術という考えを生じ、芸術の社会的機能だけでなく、主題によるいかなる分類をも否定した。

[C] 機械的な複製時代の芸術を分析することで、私たちはある非常に重要な洞察に至る。つまり、世界史上初めて、機械的な複製によって、芸術作品はその儀式への依存から解放されるということである。例えば、写真のネガからは、何枚でも複製を作り出すことができる。「本物」の複製を求めることは、意味がなくなる。しかし、本物であることの基準が芸術の製作に当てはまらなくなるとすぐに、芸術の機能全体がくつがえる。儀式に基づく代わりに、芸術はもう1つの慣習、すなわち政治に基づき始める。

[D] 芸術作品は、様々なレベルで受け取られて、評価される。2つの正反対のタイプが際立つようになる。1つでは、崇拝的な価値が重視され、もう1つでは、その作品の展示的価値が重視される。

語彙リスト

means	名	手段
reproduction	名	複製
photography	名	写真
simultaneously	副	同時に
doctrine	名	主義
for one's sake	熟	～のために
give rise to	熟	生じる
categorize	動	分類する
insight	名	洞察
free A from B	熟	AをBから解放する
negative	名	（写真の）ネガ
make sense	熟	意味をなす
the instant S′ V′	接	S′がV′するとすぐに
cease to be ～	熟	～でなくなる
applicable	形	あてはまる
reverse	動	くつがえす
stand out	熟	際立つ
exhibition	名	展示

▸単語10回CHECK 1 2 3 4 5 6 7 8 9 10

構文図解

Artistic production begins ［with ceremonial objects destined to serve
S　一般人を指す　V　M　過去分詞の名詞修飾
in a cult］. One may assume 〈that what mattered was their existence,
S　V　名詞節のthat　関係代名詞のwhat　O
not their being on view〉. The deer （portrayed by the man of the
B, not A「AではなくてB」　S　過去分詞の名詞修飾　M
Stone Age on the walls of his cave） was an instrument （of magic）. He
強調の助動詞did　the deerを指す　V　C　the deerを指す　M　S
did expose it ［to his fellow men］, but ［in the main］ it was meant ［for
V　O　M　M　S　V　M
the spirits］. Today the cult value would seem to demand 〈that the
M　S　V　名詞節のthat　O
work of art remain hidden〉. Certain statues （of gods） are accessible
demand that ～の中なのでV原形　S　M　V　C
［only to the priest in the temple］; certain sculptures （on medieval
M　S　M
cathedrals） are invisible ［to the spectator］ （on ground level）. ［When
V　C　M　M　M
these various art practices are freed from ritual］, the opportunities
特定の神の像を聖職者だけが見れたりすること　形式主語のit　S　不定詞 名詞的用法
（for exhibition of their products） are increased. It is easier 〈to exhibit
M　V　S　V　C　不定詞 名詞的用法
a portrait bust that can be sent here and there than to exhibit the
関係代名詞のthat　S′
statue of a god that has its fixed place in the interior of a temple〉.
関係代名詞のthat
寺にある神の彫像を展示するより、あちこちに送ることのできる半身像を展示するほうが簡単なこと
The same holds ［for the painting］ ［as against the mosaic or fresco
S　V　M　M
that preceded it］.
関係代名詞のthat　the paintingを指す

本文訳

芸術作品は、儀式の中で役割を果たすために用意された、儀式用のものから始まる。人は当然、重要なのはそれが展示されていることではなく、その存在だと考えるかもしれない。石器時代の人が洞窟の壁に描いた鹿は、魔術のための道具だった。彼は、それを仲間たちに実際に見せたが、主にそれは霊魂のためのものだった。今日では、その崇拝的な価値は、芸術作品が隠されたままであることが求められているように思えるだろう。特定の神の彫像は、寺院の聖職者しか目にすることができない。中世の大聖堂の特定の神の彫刻は、地上にいる観覧者は見ることができない。これらの様々な芸術的慣習が儀式から解放されると、その作品の展示の機会が増える。寺院の内部の固定された場所にある神の像を展示することより、あちこちに送ることのできる半身像を展示するほうが簡単だ。先に存在していたモザイク画やフレスコ画に対して、同じこと（あちこちに送ることができて簡単であること）が絵画に当てはまる。

語彙リスト

☐	ceremonial	形 儀式の
☐	destined to do	熟 ～する運命である
☐	serve	動 役立つ
☐	assume	動 ～を当然と思う
☐	deer	名 鹿
☐	portray	動 描く
☐	cave	名 洞窟
☐	instrument	名 道具
☐	expose A to B	熟 AをBに見せる
☐	accessible	形 接近できる
☐	sculpture	名 彫刻
☐	medieval	形 中世の
☐	cathedral	名 大聖堂
☐	invisible	形 見えない
☐	portrait	名 肖像画
☐	bust	名 半身像
☐	hold for	熟 ～に当てはまる
☐	as against	熟 ～に対して
☐	mosaic	名 モザイク画
☐	fresco	名 フレスコ画
☐	precede	動 先行する

▸単語10回CHECK 1 ☐ 2 ☐ 3 ☐ 4 ☐ 5 ☐ 6 ☐ 7 ☐ 8 ☐ 9 ☐ 10 ☐

[A] The uniqueness of a work of art is inseparable from its being part of the fabric of tradition. This tradition itself is thoroughly alive and extremely changeable. An ancient statue of Venus, for example, stood in a different traditional context with the Greeks, who made it an object of worship, than with the priests of the Middle Ages, who viewed it as a frightening idol. They both, however, had to face up to its uniqueness, that is, its aura. We know that the earliest art works originated in the service of a ritual — first the magical, then the religious kind. It is significant that the existence of the work of art with reference to its aura was never entirely separated from its ritual function. In other words, the unique value of the "authentic" work of art has its basis in ritual.

[B] This ritualistic basis, however remote, is still recognizable even in the most irreligious forms of the cult of beauty. However this secular cult of beauty, developed during the Renaissance and prevailing for three centuries, clearly showed how art's ritualistic basis was declining. With the discovery of the first truly revolutionary means of reproduction, photography, simultaneously with the rise of socialism, art sensed the approaching crisis which has become evident a century later. At the time, art reacted with the doctrine of "art for art's sake." This gave rise to the idea of "pure" art, which not only denied any social function of art but also any categorizing by subject matter.

[C] An analysis of art in the age of mechanical reproduction leads us to an all-important insight: for the first time in world history, mechanical reproduction frees the work of art from its dependence on ritual. From a photographic negative, for example, one can make any number of prints; to ask for the "authentic" print makes no sense. But the instant the standard of authenticity ceases to be applicable to artistic production, the total function of art is reversed. Instead of being based on ritual, it begins to be based on another practice: politics.

[D] Works of art are received and valued on different levels. Two opposite types stand out; with one, the accent is on the cult value; with the other, on the exhibition value of the work. Artistic production begins with ceremonial objects destined to serve in a cult. One may assume that what mattered was their existence, not their being on view. The deer portrayed by the man of the Stone Age on the walls of his cave was an instrument of magic. He did expose it to his fellow men, but in the main it was meant for the spirits. Today the cult value would seem to demand that the work of art remain hidden. Certain statues of gods are accessible only to the priest in the temple; certain sculptures on medieval cathedrals are invisible to the spectator on ground level. When these various art practices are freed from ritual, the opportunities for exhibition of their products are increased. It is easier to exhibit a portrait bust that can be sent here and there than to exhibit the statue of a god that has its fixed place in the interior of a temple. The same holds for the painting as against the mosaic or fresco that preceded it.

▸音読10回CHECK 1 2 3 4 5 6 7 8 9 10

背景知識が
広がるコラム

BACKGROUND KNOWLEDGE

複製技術時代の芸術

本問でも重要表現として、an all-important insightで紹介された考えを収めた本は、**『複製技術時代の芸術』**と言われます。ドイツの文芸批評家ヴァルター・ベンヤミンが1936年に著した本です。

この著書の中で、本文にもあったように、「**世界史上初めて、機械的な複製は芸術作品を儀式への依存から解き放った**」とベンヤミンは書きました。そして、**優れた芸術作品に対して、人々が抱く畏怖や崇拝の念**を「**aura（オーラ）**」という言葉を用いて表しました。この「**オーラ**」が根底にあってこそ、**魔術や儀式と芸術は結び付いて**きました。**複製芸術の登場**によって、**芸術が儀式から解放**されて、「**オーラ**」が失われると共に、「**儀式に基づく代わりに、芸術はもう1つの慣習である政治に基づき始める**」という大きな変化が起きました。

儀式の基盤を失った芸術は、「**芸術のための芸術**」を求めて、宗教から政治に軸を移していきました。結果として、主に映画を使って「**芸術のための芸術**」の礼拝的価値を作り、人々を戦争へと導く**ファシズム**が生まれました。これは、**政治の芸術化**と呼ばれます。ベンヤミンは、「**芸術のための芸術**」を反ファシズムの観点から批判しました。

ちなみに、「**芸術のための芸術**」は、19世紀初頭からフランスで用いられた表現です。芸術とは、「**真の**」**芸術であれば、道徳的あるいは実用的な機能とも切り離されたもの**だという考えです。

「**芸術のための芸術**」は、**芸術の価値は何らかの道徳や教訓的な目的に奉仕するという考えと対をなすもの**です。**芸術は芸術として価値**があり、**芸術の探求は、それ自体が正当化されるもの**だと主張されます。この考えが**ファシズム**を生み出すという皮肉な結果を招いたために、批判を集めることにもなりました。

ちなみに、**ファシズム**とは、20世紀初頭から中盤にかけて、**イタリアのムッソリーニとその国家ファシスト党が提唱した思想やイデオロギー・政治運動のこと**を言います。独裁的な権力、反抗の弾圧と産業や商取引のコントロールなどが行われました。

問題 10

社 会

動物の高度な認知能力

別冊p.42 ／制限時間25分／ 565 words

解答

1 ・大気と水の境界で生じる屈折を補正して、獲物に向かって水流を噴射する能力。
・獲物との距離を測って、水流の噴射を、獲物に当たる直前に最大の威力にする能力。
・獲物の軌道が変わるときでさえ、噴射した水を標的に命中させる能力。

2 本当の意味での脳ではなく、その神経密度は、約96万個の神経細胞の集まりで、数も相対的な大きさも、ほとんどの脊椎(せきつい)動物よりはるかに及ばないが、学習能力、子育て、分業、情報共有ができる高い認知能力を備えた小さな脳のようなものという意味で用いている。

3 いずれにせよ、脊椎動物よりずっと小さなミツバチの脳が、脊椎動物に匹敵する認知プロセス、あるいは少なくともその行動に対する根本的な制限になっているようには思えない。哺乳動物とミツバチの類似点は驚くべきものだが、それらに相同(そうどう)の神経系の発達の痕跡を見出すことはできない。ミツバチの神経構造がいまだに未知のものである限り、私たちはその類似性の原因を特定できない。

解説

1

下線部(a)は、**other spectacular examples**「**他の目を見張るような例**」の意味。

論理 POINT ⑤ 複数名詞は抽象の目印

複数名詞は抽象表現の一種で、その後ろに**具体例が続くことがある**ので、次の文との間に「**例えば**」と補って、見えない文のつながりを見抜きましょう。特に、**段落1行目の後半部分に登場することが多い**です。

本問でも、**other spectacular examplesが抽象表現**で、この後に認知能力がある動物の具体例であるthe Matable antの「他の」注目すべき例が登場する。次の文の**The banded archerfish「テッポウウオ」**が主人公で、その狩りの能力を3点、箇条書きにする。まず、第2段落第2文は、「**大気と水の境界で生じる屈折を補正して、獲物に向かって水流を噴射すること**」。同段落第3文は、「**獲物との距離を測って、その噴射が、獲物に当たる直前に最大の威力となること**」。同段落第4文は、「**獲物の軌道が変わるときでさえ、噴射した水を標的に命中させることができること**」となる。以上の3点が正解になる。

2

下線部(b)は**minibrains「非常に小さい脳」**という意味なので、**どういう点で「非常に小さい」のか**を、本文の記述を基に説明する。

第3段落第3文「その神経密度は昆虫の中では最も高いものの1つで、約96万個の神経細胞があるが、どの脊椎動物よりはるかに少ない」、**同段落第4文「その相対的な脳の大きさは、ほとんどの脊椎動物より小さい」**が、その説明に当たる。

一方で、**同段落第2文「本当の意味での脳ではない」**にもかかわらず、**どういった点で「脳」と呼べるのか**も、本文の記述を基に説明する。**同段落第6・7文「異なる花から、花粉や蜜の抽出方法を学習して、子供の面倒を見て、仕事の分業、尻振りダンスで離れたところにある食料や水の場所や質を教え合う」という高度な認知能力を備えているので、「脳」と呼べる**ことがわかる。

以上をまとめると、「**本当の意味での脳ではなく、その神経密度は、約96万個の神経細胞の集まりで、数も相対的な大きさも、ほとんどの脊椎動物よりはるかに及ばないが、学習能力、子育て、分業、情報共有ができる高い認知能力を備えた小さな脳のようなものという意味で用いている**」が正解。

3

構文図解①

[In any case], the much smaller brain (of the bee) does not appear to be a fundamental limitation (for comparable cognitive processes, or at least their performance).

（much：比較級の強調「ずっと」／In any case：M／the much smaller brain：S／of the bee：M／does not appear to be：V／a fundamental limitation：C／for comparable cognitive processes, or at least their performance：M）

下線部(c)の第1文**in any case**は「**いずれにせよ**」の意味の熟語。**muchは比較級smallerの強調**で「**ずっと**」の意味。比較級である以上、「**何と比べているか**」の視点で考えると、**第3段落第3文、第4文より脊椎動物との比較**とわかる。**appear to be C**は「**Cのように思える**」の意味。まとめると、「**いずれにせよ、脊椎動物よりずっと小さなミツバチの脳が、脊椎動物に匹敵する認知プロセス、あるいは少なくともその行動に対する根本的な制限になっているようには思えない**」となる。最大のポイントは、**comparableの訳出**になる。

語彙 POINT ❻ comparableの訳出

comparableはcompareの形容詞なので、直訳すると「**比較できる**」になりますが、**限定用法（名詞を修飾する用法）で使用された場合**に、「**何と比較できるか**」を明示する必要があります。例をご覧ください。

（例）

a personal computer of **comparable** size

訳 **同等の**大きさのパソコン

comparableは「**比較できる**」から、「**同等の**」という意味で使われて、「**何と同等なのか**」を文脈で明らかにする必要があります。

本問では、やはり「**脊椎動物**」になるので、**comparable**を「**脊椎動物に匹敵する**」と訳出する。

構文図解②

The similarities (between mammals and bees) are astonishing,
S M V C

▼The similaritiesを指す

but they cannot be traced [to homologous neurological developments].
S V M

butの後ろのtheyは**The similaritiesを指している**。**be traced to**は「**〜まで跡をたどる**」が直訳だが、この文では「**〜の痕跡を見出す**」と意訳する。まとめると、「**哺乳動物とミツバチの類似点は驚くべきものだが、それらに、相同の神経学的発達の痕跡を見出すことはできない**」となる。**homologousは語源を知らないと訳出が厳しい単語**なので、整理する。

語彙 POINT ⑦ homoは「同一の」の意味

homogeneous「**同質の**」／**homosexual**「**同性愛の**」／**homologous**「**相同する**」

homoは「**同一の**」という意味なので、**homogeneous**「**同質の**」、**homosexual** = **homo**「**同一の**」+ **sexual**「**性別の**」=「**同性愛の**」、**homologous**「**相同する**」となります。「**相同する**」とは、生物学の用語で、**人の手や鳥の翼のように、見た目が違っていても、その器官の発生や作りが等しいこと**を指します。

構文図解③

[As long as the animal's neural architecture remains unknown], we cannot determine the cause (of their similarity).
M S V O M

As long as「**〜する限り**」で、unknownまでの副詞節を作り、cannot determineを修飾する。**ここでのthe animal**は「**ミツバチ**」を指すので、「**ミツバチの神経構造がいまだに未知のものである限り、私たちはその類似性の原因を特定できない**」と訳す。**determine**は直訳すると「決定する」だが、この文では**the cause**「**原因**」**が目的語**なので「**特定する**」と意訳する。

1 環境 2 生物 3 生物 4 環境 5 健康 6 文化 7 学問 8 生物 9 文化 10 社会

構文図解

Various doctrines (of human cognitive superiority) are made
S M V
plausible [by a comparison of human beings and the chimpanzees].
C M 人間の認知能力の優位性を人間とチンパンジーの比較で妥当だとしていること
[For questions of evolutionary cognition], this focus is one-sided.
M S V C
Consider the evolution (of cooperation in social insects, such as the
V O M マタベレアリのような社交的なアリのこと
Matabele ant). [After a termite attack], these ants provide medical
M S V O
services. [Having called for help by means of a chemical signal],
分詞構文 M
injured ants are brought back [to the nest]. Their increased chance
S V M S
(of recovery) benefits the entire colony. Red forest ants have the
M V O S V O
ability (to perform simple arithmetic operations and to convey the
不定詞 形容詞的用法 M to perform ～と to convey ～の接続
results to other ants).

[When it comes to adaptations in animals that require sophisticated
M 関係代名詞のthat
neural control], evolution offers other spectacular examples. The
S V O S
banded archerfish is able to spit a stream (of water) [at its prey],
V O M M
[compensating for refraction at the boundary between air and
分詞構文 The banded archerfishを指す M
water]. It can also track the distance (of its prey), [so that the jet
S V O M 「結果として～」 M
develops its greatest force just before impact]. Laboratory
S
experiments show ⟨that the banded archerfish spits on target even
V 名詞節のthat O
when the trajectory of its prey varies⟩.

本文訳

人間の認知能力の優位性に関する様々な学説は、人間とチンパンジーの比較によって、妥当なものとされてきた。進化認知学の様々な疑問に対して、この焦点の当て方は偏っている。マタベレアリのような*群居する昆虫の共同作業の進化を考えてみよう。シロアリの攻撃の後に、これらのアリは医療行為を行う。化学的信号によって助けを求めた後に、傷ついたアリは、巣に連れ戻される。それらの回復可能性が高まることで、コロニー全体に利益をもたらす。ヨーロッパアカヤマアリは、単純な算数の計算をして、その結果を他のアリに伝えることができる。

動物における精巧な神経のコントロールを必要とする適応に関しては、進化によって他にも目を見張るような例を見ることができる。テッポウウオは大気と水の境界で生じる屈折を補正して、獲物に向かって水流を吐き出すことができる。それはまた、その獲物の距離を探知することもできるので、結果としてその噴射は、的中する直前に最大の威力になる。室内実験によって、テッポウウオは、その獲物の軌道が変わるときでさえ、水を噴射して標的に命中させることがわかっている。

*「群居する」とは、同種の生物がたくさん集まって生活すること。

語彙リスト

doctrine	名 学説	sophisticated	形 精巧な
cognitive	形 認知の	neural	形 神経の
superiority	名 優位性	spectacular	形 目を見張るような
plausible	形 妥当な	banded archerfish	名 テッポウウオ
insect	名 昆虫	spit	動 吐き出す
termite	名 シロアリ	stream	名 流れ
by means of	熟 ～によって	prey	名 獲物
bring back	熟 ～を連れ戻す	compensate for	熟 補正する
colony	名 コロニー	refraction	名 屈折
arithmetic	名 算数	boundary	名 境界
operation	名 演算	jet	名 噴出
convey	動 ～を伝える	laboratory	名 研究室
adaptation	名 適応	trajectory	名 軌道

▸単語10回CHECK 1 2 3 4 5 6 7 8 9 10

構文図解

Spit hunting is a technique (that requires the same timing used in
S V C 関係代名詞のthat M 分詞の後置修飾
throwing, an activity otherwise regarded as unique in the animal
同格のカンマ 分詞の後置修飾
kingdom). [In human beings], the development (of throwing) has led
M S M V
to an enormous further development (of the brain). And the
O M
archerfish? The calculations (required for its extraordinary hunting
S 分詞の後置修飾 M
technique) are based on the interplay (of about six neurons). Neural
V O M S
mini-networks could therefore be much more widespread [in the
V 比較級の強調「ずっと」 C M
animal kingdom] [than previously thought].
M they (= neural mini-networks) wereの省略

Research (on honeybees) has brought [to light] the cognitive
S M V M O
capabilities (of minibrains). Honeybees have no brains [in the real
M S V O M
sense]. Their neuronal density, however, is [among the highest in
S M V 「～の1つ」 M
insects], [with roughly 960 thousand neurons — far fewer than any
M 比較級の強調「はるかに」
vertebrate]. [Even if the brain size of honeybees is normalized to
M
their body size], their relative brain size is lower [than most
S V C M
vertebrates]. Insect behavior should be less complex, less flexible,
S V C
and less modifiable [than vertebrate behavior]. But honeybees learn
M S V
quickly 〈how to extract pollen and nectar from a large number of
M 「～する方法」 O
different flowers〉.

本文訳

水の噴射による狩猟は、投げるときに使われるのと同じタイミングを必要とする技術で、それ以外では動物界で唯一だとみなされる運動だ。人間は、投げることが発達したことで、脳がさらに大きく進化した。では、テッポウウオはどうだろう。その並外れた狩猟技術に必要とされる計算は、およそ6つの神経細胞の相互作用に基づいている。それゆえ、神経のミニネットワークは、以前考えられていたより、動物界のずっと広範囲に及んでいる可能性がある。

ミツバチの研究は、小型脳の認知能力を明るみに出した。ミツバチには、本当の意味での脳がない。しかし、その神経網の密度は昆虫の中では最も高いものの1つで、およそ96万個の神経細胞があるが、どの脊椎動物よりもはるかに少ない。たとえ、ミツバチの脳の大きさが体の大きさに標準化されていたとしても、その相対的な脳の大きさは、ほとんどの脊椎動物よりも小さいものだ。昆虫の行動は、脊椎動物の行動よりも複雑ではなく、柔軟性もなく、修正可能なものでもないはずだ。しかし、ミツバチは多数の異なる花から、花粉や蜜を抽出する方法を素早く学習する。

語彙リスト

otherwise	副	そうでなければ
regard A as B	熟	AをBとみなす
kingdom	名	王国
calculation	名	計算
extraordinary	形	並外れた
interplay	名	相互作用
honeybee	名	ミツバチ
bring O to light	熟	Oを明るみに出す
capability	名	能力
density	名	密度
among	前	～の1つ
roughly	副	およそ
vertebrate	名	脊椎動物
normalize	動	標準化する
flexible	形	柔軟な
modifiable	形	修正できる
extract	動	抽出する
pollen	名	花粉
nectar	名	蜜(みつ)

▸単語10回CHECK 1 2 3 4 5 6 7 8 9 10

構文図解

honeybeesを指す

They care for their young, organize the distribution (of tasks), and, [with the help of the waggle dance], they inform each other [about the location and quality of distant food and water].

ミツバチが子供の面倒を見て、分業を行い、遠くにある食べ物や水の場所や質を教えられる能力のこと

Early research (by Karl von Frisch) suggested 〈that such abilities cannot be the result of inflexible information processing and rigid behavioral programs〉. Honeybees learn and they remember. The most recent experimental research has, [in confirming this conclusion], created an astonishing picture (of the honeybee's cognitive competence). Their representation (of the world) does not consist entirely of associative chains. It is far more complex, flexible, and integrative. Honeybees show context-dependent learning and remembering, and even some forms (of concept formation). Bees are able to classify images [based on such abstract features as bilateral symmetry and radial symmetry]; they can comprehend landscapes [in a general way], and spontaneously come to classify new images. They have recently been promoted [to the set of species capable of social learning and tool use].

名詞節のthat / Honeybeesを指す / ミツバチに学習能力と記憶能力があること / Their representationを指す / 部分否定 / 分詞構文 / such A as B / Beesを指す / Beesを指す / 形容詞の後置修飾

本文訳

ミツバチは子供たちの面倒を見て、仕事の分業を行い、尻振りダンスの助けを借りて、離れたところにある食料や水の場所や質を、お互いに知らせ合う。

カール・フォン・フリッシュによる初期の研究では、そのような能力は、柔軟性のない情報処理や固定した行動プログラムの結果生じるのはありえないことが示唆されていた。ミツバチは、学習して記憶するのだ。最も最近の実験的研究で、この結論を確認する際に、ミツバチの認知能力について驚くべき全体像が作られた。ミツバチの世界の描写は、すべてが連想を結合させていくことで成り立っているわけではない。それは、はるかに複雑で、柔軟性があり、統合的だ。ミツバチは、状況依存の学習と記憶、そしてある種の概念形成すら示す。ミツバチは、目に入ってくる像を、左右相称や*放射相称のような抽象的な特徴に基づいて、分類することができる。すなわち、ミツバチは、風景を大まかに理解して、自発的に新しい像を分類するようになる。ミツバチは最近、社会学習や道具使用が可能な種のグループへと昇格した。

*「放射相称」は、ウニやクラゲのように、生物体の中心軸を通る相称面が3つ以上あること。

語彙リスト

care for	熟 世話をする
distribution	名 分配
waggle dance	名 尻振りダンス
location	名 場所
processing	名 処理
rigid	形 固定した
confirm	動 確認する
conclusion	名 結論
astonishing	形 驚くべき
competence	名 能力
representation	名 描写
not entirely	副 すべてが~なわけではない
associative	形 連想の
integrative	形 統一的な
classify	熟 ~を分類する
abstract	形 抽象的な
bilateral symmetry	名 左右相称
radial symmetry	名 放射相称
comprehend	動 理解する
landscape	名 景色
spontaneously	副 自発的に

▶単語10回CHECK 1 2 3 4 5 6 7 8 9 10

構文図解

[In any case], the much smaller brain (of the bee) does not appear to be a fundamental limitation (for comparable cognitive processes, or at least their performance). The similarities (between mammals and bees) are astonishing, but they cannot be traced [to homologous neurological developments]. [As long as the animal's neural architecture remains unknown], we cannot determine the cause (of their similarity).

In any case: M / the much smaller brain: S (much: 比較級の強調「ずっと」) / of the bee: M / does not appear: V / to be a fundamental limitation: C / for comparable cognitive processes, or at least their performance: M

The similarities: S / between mammals and bees: M / are: V / astonishing: C / they: S (The similaritiesを指す) / cannot be traced: V / to homologous neurological developments: M

As long as the animal's neural architecture remains unknown: M / we: S / cannot determine: V / the cause: O / of their similarity: M (their: 哺乳類とミツバチの類似性)

本文訳

いずれにせよ、脊椎動物よりずっと小さなミツバチの脳が、脊椎動物に匹敵する認知プロセス、あるいは少なくともその行動に対する根本的な制限になっているようには思えない。哺乳動物とミツバチの類似点は驚くべきものだが、それらに、相同の神経系の発達の痕跡を見出すことはできない。ミツバチの神経構造がいまだに未知のものである限り、私たちはその類似性の原因を特定できない。

語彙リスト

in any case	熟	いずれにせよ
similarity	名	類似点
be traced to	熟	～まで跡をたどる
homologous	形	相同の
neurological	形	神経系の
as long as	接	～する限り
architecture	名	構造

▸単語10回CHECK 1 2 3 4 5 6 7 8 9 10

Various doctrines of human cognitive superiority are made plausible by a comparison of human beings and the chimpanzees. For questions of evolutionary cognition, this focus is one-sided. Consider the evolution of cooperation in social insects, such as the Matabele ant. After a termite attack, these ants provide medical services. Having called for help by means of a chemical signal, injured ants are brought back to the nest. Their increased chance of recovery benefits the entire colony. Red forest ants have the ability to perform simple arithmetic operations and to convey the results to other ants.

When it comes to adaptations in animals that require sophisticated neural control, evolution offers other spectacular examples. The banded archerfish is able to spit a stream of water at its prey, compensating for refraction at the boundary between air and water. It can also track the distance of its prey, so that the jet develops its greatest force just before impact. Laboratory experiments show that the banded archerfish spits on target even when the trajectory of its prey varies. Spit hunting is a technique that requires the same timing used in throwing, an activity otherwise regarded as unique in the animal kingdom. In human beings, the development of throwing has led to an enormous further development of the brain. And the archerfish? The calculations required for its extraordinary hunting technique are based on the interplay of about six neurons. Neural mini-networks could therefore be much more widespread in the animal kingdom than previously thought.

Research on honeybees has brought to light the cognitive capabilities of minibrains. Honeybees have no brains in the real sense. Their neuronal density, however, is among the highest in insects, with roughly 960 thousand neurons — far fewer than any vertebrate. Even if the brain size of honeybees is normalized to their body size, their relative brain size is lower than most vertebrates. Insect behavior should be less complex, less flexible, and less modifiable than vertebrate behavior. But honeybees learn quickly how to extract pollen and nectar from a large number of different flowers. They care for their young, organize the distribution of tasks, and, with the help of the waggle dance, they inform each other about the location and quality of distant food and water.

Early research by Karl von Frisch suggested that such abilities cannot be the result of inflexible information processing and rigid behavioral programs. Honeybees learn and they remember. The most recent experimental research has, in confirming this conclusion, created an astonishing picture of the honeybee's cognitive competence. Their representation of the world does not consist entirely of associative chains. It is far more complex, flexible, and integrative. Honeybees show context-dependent learning and remembering, and even some forms of concept formation. Bees are able to classify images based on such abstract features as bilateral symmetry and radial symmetry; they can comprehend landscapes in a general way, and spontaneously come to classify new images. They have recently been promoted to the set of species capable of social learning and tool use.

In any case, the much smaller brain of the bee does not appear to be a fundamental limitation for comparable cognitive processes, or at least their performance. The similarities between mammals and bees are astonishing, but they cannot be traced to homologous neurological developments. As long as the animal's neural architecture remains unknown, we cannot determine the cause of their similarity.

▸音読10回CHECK 1 2 3 4 5 6 7 8 9 10

背景知識が広がるコラム

BACKGROUND KNOWLEDGE

高度な認知能力を持つ動物

近年、**動物の高度な認知能力**の発見が相次いでおり、それらが英語の論文で発表されて、多くの大学の入試問題の題材になっています。**認知能力**とは、**外界の事象に接した感覚器官の働きに、経験などの力を加えて知識を得たり、何らかの判断を下したりする能力**のことを言います。

本問で登場したような**ミツバチのダンス**に加えて、問題2に登場した**ザトウクジラの歌**が注目されています。

その他にも、**道具を使用する**動物に注目が集まっています。類人猿の**オランウータン、チンパンジー、そしてゴリラなども道具を使う**ことがわかっています。具体的には、**木の枝を「道具」にして、蜂の巣から蜂蜜を上手に採取**します。

また、ニューカレドニアに生息する**カレドニアカラス**には、**道具を使う高度な能力**と**問題解決能力が備わっている**として、注目が集まっています。カレドニアカラスは**くちばしで枝や葉から複雑な道具を作り出し、倒木の中や草木の隙間に潜む昆虫などを釣り上げる特性**を持っています。

インドネシア沖に生息する**メジロダコ**は、**ココナッツの殻を持ち歩き、危険を感じると中に隠れて身を守る習性**を見せました。**タコが道具を使用できる**ということが、大きな驚きとともに報じられました。

おわりに

本書を最後まで読んでくださった読者の方一人一人に、心より御礼申し上げます。本書は、この本の前身となる**『大学入試　レベル別英語長文問題ソリューション』**の**音読がしやすい短めの語数の長文を揃えるという特長を維持**しつつ、さらに**扱うテーマを最新のものに厳選**することで、**志望校の過去問演習に入る直前の1冊**をイメージして執筆しました。

試験本番の1週間前でも終われるように、問題数はあえて10題に限定しています。

問題を解いて、**解説を読んで終わりの長文の勉強は、もう終わり**にしましょう。重要なのは**1つの長文を自分のものにして先に進むこと**。**出てきた単語を必ず覚えて、10回音読すること**です。必要なのは、**皆さんの能動的な姿勢**です。

本書はトップレベルという最高峰のレベルなので、本書の10の英文を完璧にしたら、もうどこの大学の長文であろうと恐れることなく、立ち向かうことができます。本シリーズが、あなたの人生を変えるシリーズとなることを願っています。

最後に、本書の企画・編集を担当してくださった（株）かんき出版の前澤美恵子様、本書の素敵なデザインを施してくださったワーク・ワンダースの鈴木智則様、本書の校正を念入りにしてくださった（株）オルタナプロの渋谷超様やその他の先生方、『ソリューション最新テーマ編』シリーズのアイデアを授けてくださった（株）A.ver教務部長の中森泰樹先生、最後までお付き合いいただいた読者の皆様に、心から御礼申しあげます。

肘井　学

【著者紹介】

肘井　学（ひじい・がく）

◉――慶應義塾大学文学部英米文学専攻卒業。全国のさまざまな予備校をへて、リクルートが主催するネット講義サービス「スタディサプリ」で教鞭をとり、高校生、受験生から英語を学びなおす社会人まで、圧倒的な満足度を誇る。

◉――「スタディサプリ」で公開される「英文読解」の講座は、年間25万人の生徒が受講する超人気講座となっている。さらに「東大英語」「京大英語」を担当し、受講者に多くの成功体験を与えている。

◉――週刊英和新聞「朝日ウィークリー（Asahi Weekly）」にてコラムを連載するなど、幅広く活躍中。

◉――著書に『大学入試 肘井学の読解のための英文法が面白いほどわかる本』『大学入試 肘井学の ゼロから英語長文が面白いほどわかる本』『大学入試 ゼロから英文法が面白いほどわかる本』『大学入試 肘井学の 作文のための英文法が面白いほどわかる本』（KADOKAWA）、『大学入試 すぐわかる英文法』『大学入試 すぐ書ける自由英作文』『大学入試 絶対できる英語リスニング』（教学社）、『高校の英文法が１冊でしっかりわかる本』『高校の英文読解が１冊でしっかりわかる本』（かんき出版）などがある。

大学入試 レベル別英語長文問題ソリューション最新テーマ編３ トップレベル

2021年11月18日　第１刷発行
2022年11月15日　第２刷発行

著　者――肘井　学
発行者――齊藤　龍男
発行所――株式会社かんき出版
東京都千代田区麴町4-1-4 西脇ビル　〒102-0083
電話　営業部：03(3262)8011㈹　編集部：03(3262)8012㈹
FAX　03(3234)4421　振替　00100-2-62304
https://kanki-pub.co.jp/

印刷所――大日本印刷株式会社

ISBN978-4-7612-3052-4 C7382